# Navigating the Unknown: Trusting God With the Results

# NAVIGATING THE UNKNOWN

## TRUSTING GOD WITH THE RESULTS

This book is about navigating the unknown,
relying on the truth of the Word of God.
I pray this book can help others when they are
facing unknown situations in their lives.

## Annie Hardy-Mack

Charleston, SC
www.PalmettoPublishing.com

*Navigating the Unknown*
Copyright © 2022 by Annie Hardy-Mack

First Edition

Paperback ISBN: 978-1-68515-532-2

Unless otherwise indicated, Scriptural quotations used in this book are from the following:
ESV Study Bible Copyright C 2008 by Crossway Publishers
KJV Life Application Study Bible Tyndale House Publishing Inc. Copyright C 1988, 1989, 1990,
1091, 1993, 1996
NIV Study Bible, Copyright C 1985, 1995, 2002, 2008 by Zondervan, Grand Rapids, Michigan
NLT Illustrated Study Bible New Living Translation, registered trademarks of Tyndale House Pub-
lishers, Inc. Copyright C 2015
The David Jeremiah Study Bible NIV Copyright C 2016 by David Jeremiah, Inc. Published by
Worthy Publishing, a division of Worthy Media, Inc.
New King James Version Copyright C 1979, 1980, 1982, by Thomas Nelson, Inc.
Wayne Dyer—Famous Inspirational Quotes
Albert Einstein----www.goodreads,com
Anne Frank—www.goodreads.com
Robert M. Hensel—https://quotefancy.com/quote/1557427
Dr. David Jeremiah, 2000 Word Publishing, Previously Titled, A Bend in the Road: Finding God
When Your World Caves In.
Dr. David Jeremiah, Tyndale House Publishing, Release Date 2013
Stateman-Nelson Mandela from Long Walk to Freedom 1994# Living the Legacy www.goodreads.com
"Healing the Soul of a Woman: How to Overcome Your Emotional Wounds," Joyce Meyer, Publish-
er, Faith Words, Released 2018
Dr. Myles Munroe, Whitaker House—Release 2019
Julian of Norwich www.azquotes.com
Mehmet Murat Iidan, Playwright and Novelist, Released 1965, Quotes.net Stand4LLC,2021WEB
10 September 2021, www.quotes.net/quote
Joel Osteen—Famous Inspirational Quotes
Patrick Overton Famous Quotes www.goodreads.com
Kristalyn Salters-Pedneault, PhD.
Ralph Waldo Emerson—Famous Inspirational Quotes www.goodreads.com
William Wordsworth—*The Excursion*
Author's Email: Navigateunk@gmail.com

# DEDICATION

I am dedicating this book to the loving memory of an amazing woman, the late Bobbie Gray, who gave me the greatest understanding of who Jesus is. No matter what the conversation was, she did not judge me. She steered me toward the Word of God because she knew no matter what I was going through, the answer was in the word.

I would have loved to present Bobbie with a copy of this book. I know she would have been happy for me. Bobbie, thank you, for believing in me.

Also, I dedicate this book to my children, Kristen, and Shawn. You are the reason I am where I am today. You always presented the best for yourselves. The love of God always shined through in your lives. You have been on this journey with me, and for that, I am profoundly proud of you. Thank you for being my biggest supporters. I love you with everything in me; I could not have done it alone.

# TABLE OF CONTENTS

# ACKNOWLEDGMENTS

I thank God for being my everything. Without His love, and His guidance, I would not have been able to navigate this journey called life. Because of His grace and mercy, and the truth of His word, I can stand today and give Him praise.

I wish both of my parents were alive so that they could share in this accomplishment with me. I know that they are watching from above and are smiling and they are wishing me well.

To my spiritual mother, Bishop Jean Bird-Taylor. I cannot put into words the love and gratitude I have for you. Thank you for seeing in me what I did not see in myself. Thank you for allowing God to use you to minister to me in my brokenness. You were a shoulder to cry on when I was burdened, an ear when I needed to vent, a counselor when I needed advice, and a disciplinarian when I needed to be corrected.

To my husband Curtis, thank you for allowing me to sit for hours and write what God has given me. Thank you for your knowledge of scriptures. You have a scripture for every trial or tribulation we face. You are a kind, loving husband, and a friend. Your encouragement means the world to me. May God bless you.

To my two wonderful blessings, my children, Shawn, and Kristin., and to my beautiful daughter-in law Elizabeth. You are my greatest joy. You are my inspiration. I love you without reservation. To my grandkids Jahshua, Janaiyah, Kaiyah, Christopher, and Jonathan. You are so special to me. I cannot imagine life without you. I love you to the moon and back.

Thank you to all my siblings; we may not talk every day, but you are always there when I call, especially my sister Celia. Thank you for all your help and your advice.

Thanks to my best friend Carla Jefferson, for all your help, patience, prayers, and encouragement through the years.

Thank you to my mentor, Rev. Lydia Patricia Ford. You have imparted wisdom into my life in such a profound way. Thank you for being accessible in times of need. Thank you for allowing me to be part of your ministries in whatever way the Lord directed you. You have been such a part of my growth in the ministry. God bless you.

Thank you to my dear friends, Rev. Dr. Marilyn Grant, Rev. Cynthia Bastiany, and Evangelist Brenda Williams and Dr. Bevon Malcolm. You have stood with me, encouraged me on this journey, and prayed me through troubled times. Thank you for always being there to give advice and for listening. But most of all for loving me just the way I am.

To the Agape Fellowship Ministries' family, I love journeying with you. What can I say about the people who showed me what true unity is all about? Apostles Eugene and Robin Taylor, I love you with the love of God. Thank you for being an example of Christ.

May God continue to bless each of you!

Annie Hardy-Mack

# INTRODUCTION

"COME TO ME, ALL YOU WHO LABOR AND ARE
HEAVY LADEN, AND I WILL GIVE YOU REST"."
MATTHEW 11:28 (NKJV) ()

The unknown is hard, it can be difficult, and it can be frightening. When you are navigating the unknown, you are moving from one place to another. You are preparing to set out on a journey of which you do not know. The unknown is like traveling a road without direction as to where you are going. One time or another, I believe that all of us have had to face times of uncertainty in our lives. The reality is that none of us is secure in this world, except in Christ Jesus. The unknown in our lives is hard and rarely welcome because it intrudes on our sense of well-being, our sense of purpose. We all have a hunger to know our future, but we do not like being in the dark and we do not like surprises.

It is the not knowing that can sometimes cause us fear and stress. We think, if we know what to expect, or what is going to happen, it will give us a measure of control over our life. But until we learn to trust God and relinquish all of our control to Him, we can become discouraged, hopeless, and filled with fear.

Therefore, trusting God with the unknown is vital. Never be afraid to trust a known God with an unknown future because trusting God does not come because we understand it, it comes because we are confident in His love, His goodness, and His mercy. I have had many seasons of challenging times navigating the unknown. One day, I was driving my granddaughter to school, and I heard the Lord say, "Navigating the Unknown: Trusting God With the Results." For days I pondered what that phrase meant.

I tried to use it as a theme for a women's conference, but the Lord said no. I even wrote a Sunday School curriculum entitled, "Navigating the Unknown." The Lord said no, "That is not it." It was not until I realized later that the Lord was directing me to author this book. I realized that often what we go through is not always about us or for us. Rather, our trials and tribulations is a lesson plan that God uses for us to minister to others. . At the time I was navigating the unknown, I did not have a clear picture of who God was.

There are countless people out there, people who have lost hope, people who are trying to navigate situations on their own just as I did, and they all have no concept of who God is.

A considerable number of people have fought so hard and for so long on their own to change their circumstances that they lash out at others who may try to help them. It could be because they feel they can no longer trust people or see anything as a blessing.

They do not see help from others as a blessing because their mental, physical, and spiritually mindset is depleted. Their physical being is depleted because they have tried to navigate on their own for so long and have not relied on help from our Lord and savior. But I promise you that as you gain your strength and go back to the right mindset and seek help from God, it will be a blessing that you shall never forget. I am not saying it will be easy, but I am saying it will be worth it.

There will be days you will ask God what you did to deserve being in your situation. Life is full of unknowns, but there is no way you would have made it this far on your own. No matter what is going on in your life, do not lose faith in God's goodness. Just navigate the unknown using God as your GPS.

# CHAPTER 1

# NAVIGATING THE UNKNOWN WITH FAITH

"NOW FAITH IS THE SUBSTANCE OF THINGS HOPE
FOR, THE EVIDENCE OF THINGS NOT SEEN."
HEBREWS 11:1 (KJV)

When living during the unknown, each day can feel like nothing more than another opportunity for you to fail. When you are facing the unknown, some days you feel powerless. The unknown can be so frightening, you do not want to get out of bed. You become fearful because you feel you are not in control of anything. Also, when fear sets in, it causes you to feel that you do not have the ability to fix your situation, to change or reverse it. One of the strategies we tend to employ when we feel fear is to keep our expectations low, so we are not disappointed by others. With the unknown, you often feel a significant loss of control, and worry can become an easy yet ineffective substitute. I encourage you, instead of viewing the day as an opportunity to fail, try looking for the blessing that the day holds. Being thankful for your blessings, rather than fearing the disappointment that may occur, can bring joy. When you are facing the unknown, stop questioning or looking for the bad, because all that it does is deplete your emotional, physical, and mental energy. Have faith as you navigate through this period of questions and wondering. Sometimes you may experience the pain of uncertainty, and about how you feel about yourself. You may begin to define yourself by your external circumstances and your fear of the unknown.

Somedays you may reflect, but reflection brings about panic because you race around looking for external circumstances to define you differently. Letting your pain, your confusion and your feelings of helplessness overwhelm you. Sometimes you can make hasty decisions, decisions to explore without the weight of your value riding on the choices you have made.

NELSON MANDELA ONCE SAID "I LEARNED THAT COURAGE WAS NOT THE ABSENCE OF FEAR, BUT THE TRIUMPH OVER IT. THE BRAVE MAN IS NOT HE WHO DOES NOT FEEL AFRAID, BUT HE WHO CONQUERS THAT FEAR."

The key to navigating the unknown is faith. If you have faith as small as a mustard seed, it is enough. Matthew 17:20 tells us "You can say to a mountain, move from here to there and it will move." Nothing is impossible for you. So instead of allowing this season of the unknown to define you, see it as an opportunity to get to know yourself better. Walk in faith. Use this time to examine the aspects of your life in a way that you have never taken time to do so before. Because during this unknown time, rarely do you see this time as a time to pause and reflect. Instead, you see it as a reflection of your failures or your unworthiness. Because faith is confidence in what we hope for and assurance about what we do not see. There are seasons in life when things do not add up. It is in those seasons that we must kickstart our faith. Faith is trusting God even when you do not understand His plan. Isaiah 55:8 says, "For my thoughts are not your thoughts, neither are your ways my ways, declares the Lord." We must trust that God knows how to become the answer to all our needs. You must be able to see and trust God in times of uncertainty, allowing God to navigate you through all the unknown times you will have in your life. To do this, you must surrender every situation to Him. You must be able to see God in the dark, especially in a world filled with accelerating, unprecedented change.

The ability to navigate the unknown and explore new areas is becoming an essential skill. Mainly because you will need to change the lens you use for seeing the unknown. You will have to ask yourself, *Do you see the unknown as something to be feared, challenged, dealt with, managed, or overcome?* Trust that God knows the outcome.

The Bible says in Isaiah 43:2, "I will be with you when you pass through the waters, and when you pass through the rivers, they will not overwhelm you. You will not be scorched when you walk through the fire, and the flame will not burn you. This is a time that you must walk by faith and not by sight."

"WHEN YOU WALK TO THE EDGE OF ALL THE LIGHT YOU HAVE AND TAKE THAT FIRST STEP INTO THE DARKNESS OF THE UNKNOWN YOU MUST BELIEVE THAT ONE OF TWO THINGS WILL HAPPEN. THERE WILL BE SOMETHING SOLID FOR YOU TO STAND UPON OR YOU WILL BE TAUGHT TO FLY."
PATRICK OVERTON

# Note to Self
## Navigating the Unknown with Faith

_____

_____

_____

_____

_____

_____

_____

_____

_____

_____

_____

_____

_____

_____

_____

_____

_____

_____

_____

_____

_____

_____

_____

# NOTE TO SELF
## NAVIGATING THE UNKNOWN WITH FAITH

_____

_____

_____

_____

_____

_____

_____

_____

_____

_____

_____

_____

_____

_____

_____

_____

_____

_____

_____

_____

_____

_____

_____

_____

_____

# CHAPTER 2

# SEEING GOD IN THE DARK

"GOD IS OUR REFUGE AND STRENGTH, A
VERY PRESENT HELP IN TROUBLE."
PSALM 46:1 (NIV)

Over the years I had to learn to trust God. I was born in a small town in Alabama. I have two brothers and four sisters. My oldest sister passed away in childbirth and left four children who came to live with my parents. I was thirteen years old at the time. At thirteen years old, I did not understand a lot about death. All I knew was something bad had happened that left my parents incredibly sad.

I believed losing a child and having to raise an additional four small kids was part of their sadness. As a thirteen-year-old child, I felt helpless. So, at the age of seventeen I left Alabama, the place I had called home, and relocated to Connecticut. I had no idea what was ahead for a young girl like me because I left behind my parents and my siblings in search of a new life. I stayed with my brother for about two years. My brother was like a father to me, and his wife was like a mother.

Being from a small town, I had to grow up fast, because I no longer had my parents to rely on for food and shelter. I did not have a driver's license or knew how to use public transportation. At seventeen I had to figure out quickly how to obtain employment. I was able to secure a job as a dietary aide at a local hospital. This job was at a mental health facility, and there I was exposed to all sorts of mental illnesses I had never heard of before.

After six months, I left the job because I could no longer function amid seeing people's daily struggle with mental illness. Stepping into the unknown again was scary. Eventually, I found employment at another hospital in town, and at this facility, I entered a nurse's aide training program.

Later I reconnected with an old high school sweetheart, dated for about a year, and we got married. I moved from one town to another. There, I found a job at an insurance company. Thank God, the job was at a walking distance from my home because I did not know anyone, not even my neighbors, and we did not have a car. I had to walk to every place I needed to go.

Before long, I was pregnant with my first child. The doctors informed me that I was pregnant in the tube and that soon I would miscarry the fetus. Talking about the unknown, I was so scared, my parents were two-thousand miles away, and my husband did not know anything about how to comfort a woman with a situation.

I do not think my husband understood the severity of our situation. Getting married at such an early age, we had no idea what to expect in a number of situations. I didn't know anything about God or how to pray about my situation. One day I went to see a doctor at the clinic, and he said I was in my third month. I said to him the other doctor said the fetus would die before I was three months. The doctor said they gave you misinformation. It was such a relief, because with this encouraging news, I could finally sleep at night. I had been so scared not knowing what to expect or when the loss of the fetus would occur. With my mind at ease, before long, I could feel the baby moving.

This was my first experience truly recognizing the goodness of God. I continued to work until my seventh month, and then, I left on maternity leave. By the time I was 20 years old, I was both a wife and mother. I had the responsibility of running a household and caring for an infant son. One day, I noticed my husband visited his friends and regularly spent time with them, while I stayed home to keep house and care for the baby.

I decided it was time to find another job so I could meet people, and I did. I got a job and remained there for about three years. While at this job, I met Mary, she was about ten years older than me. We became friends. She would baby-sit for me while I went for medical appointments, the grocery store, or for some me-time.

This lady was a saving grace to me because I did not have family near who I could count on to help me. She had one daughter who was grown and living on her own. My husband had received his driver's license and we had gotten a car. When I did my shopping, I would pick up my friend and we would go to the malls and other places. I was so glad to have her in my life, especially, because one day, I felt sick, she encouraged me to see the doctor and he said I was expecting another baby. I thought, *Oh no, I am struggling as it is. Trying to be a wife and mother and working full time, what am I going to do?*

My friend Mary often said to me it is all going to work out. I thought, *Oh well I better get prepared*. I did not know how to pray, so I started having conversations with my unborn baby every day. I would tell her that she had a big brother and that she would have someone to play with soon.

At twenty-seven weeks, I went into labor and had a premature baby girl. She was two-and-a-half pounds at birth and had to stay in the incubator for about eight weeks. Soon she came home, and I had additional responsibilities caring for another child. After a few weeks of being home from the hospital, she started crying constantly. I had to take her back to the doctor and he found she had double hernias and needed to undergo surgery at twelve-weeks old.

My first child was six years old by now. Even though he loved his little sister, he was so jealous of her, as she got so much of my time due to her illness.

Over the years, my husband and I drifted apart. He had become verbally abusive, and he found every excuse to stay away from home. I did not understand that he was a young father with two kids and a wife, and he himself had no idea how to deal with the changes in his life. We tried marriage counseling, which did not work, so twenty-five years after marriage, it all crashed and burned, divorce came. Neither he nor I had any interest in trying to keep something alive that obviously had died long ago. Talking about the unknown, and seeing God in the dark, for the first time, I was going to be on my own, having to find my own way in life and take care of two adult children. The oldest was in third year of college and the youngest was in the middle of her first year of nursing school.

I have always been one of those people who stayed to myself. I did not know a lot about what goes on out there in this big, wide world. I had been a homebody. Now at forty-four years old and financially responsible for myself, I had to re-enter a world that I truly knew little about. Talking about the unknown, I started to feel hopeless, depressed, and as a failure.

One day I realized I needed to make some different decisions in my life. I had to make some choices that may not be pleasing to others, but it was now or never. I announced to my two adult children that they were now on their own. If they were going to make it through college, it was on their dime. I enrolled myself in college, with the intention of securing a degree in business administration. I worked eight hours per day and went to school at night. Turned out, that was the best decision I ever made. One reason is I met some people who have become life-long friends.

Some years later, I sought counseling. I took a hard look at myself and decided to join a prominent church in the area. Aside from attending Sunday morning worship, I started to become involved in Sunday School and Bible Study. At this church, I met someone who would really change my life—my Sunday School Teacher, Bobbie. We started to talk about a lot of things, but what Bobbie taught me was something that I had never heard about before. And that was Proverb 3:5-6 that said, "Trust in the Lord with all your heart, lean not to your own understanding, in all your ways acknowledge Him, and He shall direct your path."

My friend was letting me know that I can no longer do things on my own, that there was someone I could count on to help me through the difficulties in my life because I was carrying around so much pain and disappointment. Now that I had heard about this person, I could not wait to get to church on Sundays, because I needed to hear more about this Jesus. Soon I learned that Jesus loves me, that He loves me so much that He gave His life for me.

I came to understand Philippians 4:13 "For I could do all things through Christ, who gives me strengthen." Another thing that I learned was that I had to forgive. And that I could no longer depend on someone else to make me happy, that my happiness depended solely on me.

As I said earlier, I did not know much about prayer. I started to listen to my friend Bobbie when she would pray in our Sunday School class. I started to pattern my prayers after what she said. Pretty soon, I added my own words. First, I would say, *Oh Father, how long. I cried for how long because I had been navigating the unknown for so long.* I started to tell the Lord what was in my heart and what was on my mind. I would tell Him how I felt about what had happen to me.

But one day I thought I may not understand God's hand in things, but it does not mean He is not working in my life. Eventually, I realized that some of those old feelings of abandonment were gone. I did not feel the loss of my marriage or the grief of that loss I had experienced for so long. I felt free. I felt like the weight of the world had been lifted from my shoulders. Before long, I had joined other auxiliaries within the ministry, and I started interacting with other people. I felt that I had something to give again, and that I truly was not a failure.

I had lived for so many years as they say with "a monkey on my back." I did not realize that the Lord had taken away all those bad feelings; I was ready to live life again. I had to learn that God can be silent when He is navigating us through the unknown because He is helping us and growing us into individuals, He wants us to be. I learned that God can and will guide us while we are blindfolded. Soon my prayer was, "Create in me a clean heart and renew in me the right spirit." All I had to do was surrender my will, my plans, my concept of control to God through voicing my fears and frustration to Him.

Then I had to request His guidance and ask Him to help me with my faith. Psalm 32:8 says, "I will instruct you and teach you in the way you should go; I will counsel you with my eye upon you." Proverb 4:13 says, "Keep hold of instruction; do not let go; guard her, for she is your life."

John 14:26 says, "But the helper, the Holy Spirit, whom the Father will send in my name, He will teach you all things and bring to your remembrance all that I have said to you."

"WHEN LIFE SUDDENLY TURNS UPSIDE DOWN, THERE, IN THE MIDST OF YOUR TRIALS AND IN THE CENTER OF YOUR PAIN, IS GOD, COMFORTING, GUIDING, ENCOURAGING, TEACHING, SUSTAINING."
DR. DAVID JEREMIAH

Prayer:
Lord, what do you want to teach me to make me a better person? What are your plans to make me more effective? Lead me and guide me through this process, O Lord. Be my teacher; show me your ways. Most of all, do not let me miss the lesson you have prepared for me. Amen.

# NOTE TO SELF
## SEEING GOD IN THE DARK

# NOTE TO SELF
## SEEING GOD IN THE DARK

_____

_____

_____

_____

_____

_____

_____

_____

_____

_____

_____

_____

_____

_____

_____

_____

_____

_____

_____

_____

_____

_____

_____

_____

# CHAPTER 3

# TRUSTING GOD WHEN YOU DO NOT UNDERSTAND THE UNKNOWN

"FOR MY THOUGHTS ARE NOT YOUR THOUGHTS,
NEITHER ARE YOUR WAYS MY WAYS, SAITH THE LORD."
ISAIAH 55:8-9 (KJV)

I will agree, trying to navigate the unknown is tough. You ask where is God when the future is uncertain? When you do not understand, it makes you question things that you have not questioned before. But what you must understand is that change is inevitable, change will happen. Change can be perceived as either good or bad. Whether positive or negative, change usually brings feelings of fear, anxiety, indecision, tension, confusion, and hopelessness. All those years after my divorce, not knowing much about God, I had spent countless dollars on anxiety medications. I lived in the fear of failure. Fear of making the wrong decision in life. I also did not understand that change happen whether or not you want it.

Often, we lose heart or vision during this time that we do not understand, because it does not appear as if anything is happening. However, I learned that you trust God with change because He is the same yesterday and forever. Also, because He is a great God. His word tells us in Jeremiah 29:11, "His plan is to prosper us and not to harm us, to give us hope and a future," because He knows the end from the beginning. Change is simply God's means for bringing us closer to our destiny, but to stay the course, it is important to know the beauty of destiny. To reach our destiny, Matthew 6:33 says, "We must first 'seek ye the kingdom of God, and His righteousness and all these things shall be added unto you.'"

Because He is always there for us, when all else fails in life, we must trust God's plan for our life. I had to immerse myself in prayer. I had to let go of thinking that I am the only one who can solve my problems. I had to come to grips with the fact that God never promised to shield me from difficulties; He only promised to be with me if I wanted Him to.

I had spent so many years blaming my first husband for not making me happy. Being angry and blaming other people did not help me to get through. It was only at this time I realized that my problem was too big for me to handle. I decided asking God to be with me would help me endure whatever situations came my way. The Bible says, in Isaiah 26:3 that, "Thou wilt keep Him in perfect peace whose mind is stayed on thee, because He trusts in thee."

One day I decided to talk to someone who could give me Godly advice. Because difficult situations seem worse when you are facing them alone. My friend Bobbie would often tell me that God does not keep us from tests and trials, He helps us get through them. I knew her experiences could help me see my situation through a different lens. I also came to understand that when things became hard, I had to let go of thinking that life should always go my way and that God answers every prayer, but He does not always answer "Yes," He will say "No" or "Wait." I had to learned to not only be happy when things went well, to enjoy each day, and to look for the good in it, but also let go of feeling entitled to a problem-free life. One day I decided to make a list of the things that I appreciated about life. Even if it was as basic as a roof over my head or food on my table, I told God I was thankful for them. Noticing the good things in life helped me to have a more positive attitude and see God's hand in all things, good or bad. I realized that tests and trials teach us what and who we are.

I came to understand that God can make us capable and strong, even when facing the unknown. I did not realize that we should think of our trials as our training and that they help us grow and learn to become more dependent on the Lord. Because sometimes, God allow us to go through difficulties in this life because it is during these times that we grow in our faith and develop more of the character God desires of us.

Scriptures teach us trials and instances where we have to prove our faith bring out endurance, steadfastness, and patience. James 1:12 says, "Blessed is the one who preservers under trial because, having stood the test, that person will receive the crown of life that the Lord has promised to those who love Him." Moreover, scriptures remind us in Romans 8:28 that, "All things work together for good to them that love God." Yet when we encounter difficulties, we often wonder, why.

Stepping into the unknown can have different meanings for everyone. The unknown can be entering a new relationship, moving to a new town or state, meeting new people, or starting a new job. Everyone goes through stages or seasons in their life, sometimes more often than others. They are unsure of what the future will hold, unsure of what they are doing, or what will happen in their situation.

When we stand on the edge of change and fear, it is then that we must reach out to God for direction and peace. Peace come with finding trust in God and His sovereignty. When we know for sure that our lives are in God's hands and that He has ultimate control, we can trust in Him because stepping into the unknown areas of our lives requires submission to God's calling and to God's will.

Jeremiah 17:7 says, "Blessed is the man who trusts in the Lord, and whose hope is the Lord."

Jeremiah 29:11 says, "For I know the plans I have for you, declares the Lord, plan to prosper you and not to harm you, plans to give you a hope and a future."

Roman 15:13 says, "Now may the God of hope fill you with all joy and peace in believing, so that you may abound in hope, through the power of the Holy Spirit."

"LIVE THE FEARLESS LIFE GOD CREATED YOU TO ENJOY!
DR. DAVID JEREMIAH

Prayer:
Father, you love me and will take care of me as you promised in your word. I lift my eyes of faith and look to you, the author and finisher of my faith. I cast my cares on you, for you care for me. I trust your plan to give me the future I hoped for. In your name I pray. Amen.

# Note to Self
## Trusting God When You Do Not
## Understand the Unknown

_____

_____

_____

_____

_____

_____

_____

_____

_____

_____

_____

_____

_____

_____

_____

_____

_____

_____

_____

_____

_____

_____

_____

_____

# NOTE TO SELF
## TRUSTING GOD WHEN YOU DO NOT
## UNDERSTAND THE UNKNOWN

_____

_____

_____

_____

_____

_____

_____

_____

_____

_____

_____

_____

_____

_____

_____

_____

_____

_____

_____

_____

_____

_____

_____

_____

_____

# CHAPTER 4

# WHEN YOU FEEL, GOD IS NOT LISTENING TO YOU

"THOSE WHO KNOW YOUR NAME TRUST IN YOU;
FOR YOU, LORD, HAVE NEVER FORSAKEN
THOSE WHO SEEK YOU."
PSALM 9:10 (NIV)

Sometimes God is silent. You may earnestly seek God, but in return only sense His silence. And His silence can be difficult, frustrating, and even excruciating. If you are feeling that God is not hearing your prayers, ask yourself if you have really said, "your will be done" instead of "my will be done." During the years of being divorced and alone, I had prayed constantly asking God to send me Mr. Right. I had outlined all the things I wanted in a man, not once asking for someone who loved or had a relationship with God. Not realizing that God's silence meant that I was not ready to have anyone in my life. I had to grow and learn that I could take care of myself with His help.

His silence meant that even the relationship that I had with Him needed to be strengthened and needed to grow to the point that my total reliance was strictly on Him and Him alone. Once I understood that, I met someone who was kind, loving, and had the biggest heart for God. Soon he and I attended Sunday School, Bible Study, and Sunday morning service together. We were inseparable. We would go to gospel concerts together; we would travel with each other's church for services or events.

One day we decided that living separate had to end. We decided to get married. We set the date and booked the reception hall. I purchased the wedding gown, and one month before our wedding, my fiancée started feeling ill and was diagnosed with throat cancer. We asked the doctors should we continue with our wedding plans, and they said, "No." Receiving this horrendous news, I experienced a gambit of emotions. One moment fear, another anger and hopelessness. Anger, that I had waited for someone like this all my life and now this. Cancer? What? I had to take a deep breath and be grateful that he was alive.

At that moment, I remembered what my friend Bobbie had said in one of our past conversations: Do not pray to God to keep you safe from the trials of life. Pray to Him to give you strength to use that trial to strengthen you. She said, when you pray, you are not always going to hear God's voice, especially when He is saying wait. But I still asked myself why was God silent, why did He allow us to go through purchasing this wedding venue if He knew it would never happen? I ask myself the question: Is there anything blocking me from being able to hear from God? I had to recognize that silence can be intimate. Silence could also be a sign of God's trust in me. I urge you, do not stop praying. Do not stop reading God's word. During God's silence, I immersed myself into my favorite verses in the Bible especially Psalm 9:10 that says, "Those who know your name put their trust in you, for you Lord, have not forsaken those who seek you."

Deuteronomy 4:29 tells us, "But from there you will seek the Lord your God and you will find Him. If you search after Him with your heart and with your soul." It takes significant effort on our part to seek God, but the Bible says you will be rewarded for that effort.

Trusting in God and believing in His word is the key. After much trial and tribulations throughout this cancer situation, my fiancée recovered, and we were able to get married. Soon God started moving me in an entirely different direction than I had ever imagined. I wanted to study to become a minister. I enrolled in a Bible class at a local cathedral in town and studied theology for about two years. In addition to the two years, I spent studying theology, I enrolled in an online course at a Bible college to continue my studies. After a couple of years, my husband encouraged me to enroll into a ministry program at a local seminary. We were enjoying our life together and had wonderful years before other symptoms of "cancer" occurred. Then one day he started to not feel well and was diagnosed with small-cell lung cancer, so the last two years of his life were filled with radiation and chemotherapy, and he died in my last year at the seminary.

My biggest regret is that he did not live to see me graduate from the program at the seminary. I understand now why God was silent. He was preparing me for what was to come. Previously I knew truly little of the Word of God. Through my study, I had come to learn of His promises.

One of His promises to His children in Psalms 121 is, "In the times of trouble we can lift our eyes to the hills from whence cometh our help." My help came "from the Lord, who made heaven and earth." Another one of His promises in Psalm 147 is "He healeth the broken in heart, and bindeth up their wounds."

One day I was in deep depression and God reminded me of one of the classes at the seminary in which each of us had to submit a dissertation. As I thought about what each student had said, I was reminded that "God will fight for you."

In class someone said, "Sometimes we may have to be like the Shulamite woman in Two Kings, Chapter four, be content, and know all is well. Walk in faith and know God can work a miracle in our lives." Another person said, "God chose us; we did not choose Him." Then I remembered my dissertation paper title was, "Where is your Faith in the Midst of the Storm." At that moment, I knew I had to stay positive and rely on His word. Positive thoughts quieted my fears and irrational thinking by helping me focus my attention on something that was stress-free, that was God's word.

Just know that hearing God's voice is by far the most important part of your prayer and fellowship time with Him. You cannot have an intimate and wonderful fellowship with God without learning to hear God's voice and intimately communicating with Him regardless of the situation. The Bible tells the story of a man name Job who was well-acquainted with God's silence. In his pain and suffering, he cried out to God. He asked for answers. And he kept asking. But for the first thirty-seven chapters of the Book of Job, his cries for God's help and relief are met only by God's deafening silence.

As Christians, we are not always going to hear God's voice, but from Job we can learn a few practical things to do when God seems silent:

- **Examine Your Life**: Begin by asking yourself—Is there any unconfessed sin in your life?
- **Accept God's Authority**: Recognize that God can be silent. There is no obligation for God to answer you, inform you, or let you know anything.
- **Listen to what God is saying**: Although God may seem silent regarding a specific request or petition, remember

that He is in constant communication with us. Search God's word to find out what He has to say about the problems you are facing or questions you are asking. Ask God to speak to you through the Holy Spirit, who lives inside you.

"WISDOM IS OFTTIMES NEARER WHEN WE
STOOP, THAN WHEN WE SOAR."
WILLIAM WORDSWORTH—*THE EXCURSION*

# NOTE TO SELF
## WHEN YOU FEEL, GOD IS NOT LISTENING TO YOU

_____

_____

_____

_____

_____

_____

_____

_____

_____

_____

_____

_____

_____

_____

_____

_____

_____

_____

_____

_____

_____

_____

_____

_____

# NOTE TO SELF
## WHEN YOU FEEL, GOD IS NOT LISTENING TO YOU

_____

_____

_____

_____

_____

_____

_____

_____

_____

_____

_____

_____

_____

_____

_____

_____

_____

_____

_____

_____

_____

_____

_____

_____

_____

# CHAPTER 5

# HINDERANCES TO HEARING GOD'S VOICE

"IF WE CONFESS OUR SINS, HE IS FAITHFUL AND
JUST AND WILL FORGIVE US OUR SINS AND
CLEANSE US FROM ALL RIGHTEOUSNESS."
1 JOHN 1:9 (KJV)

There are many things that can hinder your ability to hear from God. Hearing God's voice is by far the most important part of your prayer and fellowship time with Him. You must seek His face to have a more intimate, more powerful relationship. However, there is a substantial difference between hearing God's voice and listening to him. The biblical word to listen means to hear God's voice reverently and attentively, with the intention of doing and obeying what you hear Him say. Our heart needs to be right with God, with no hinderances to hearing His voice.

After years of being a widow. I thought I wanted to start dating again, not realizing that dating in 2016 was different from dating in the seventies, eighties, or even the nineties. Forgetting that men no longer walk the lady to the door or kiss her hand and say goodnight. Before long I found myself amidst fornication and sin. Not realizing that sin is a huge hindrance to hearing the voice of God, because

God does not abide in sin. The only thing I could hear at this point was God's conviction. I had to learn to deal with my sin if I wanted to return to that intimate fellowship with God.

I had to learn that walking in disobedience always blocks us from hearing more from God. In His mercy, He does not let us bypass our sin and begins to speak to us about other things. I had to remember God's word, where He says, "For the wages of sin is death; but the gift of God is eternal life through Jesus Christ our Lord."

Also, His word said, in 1 John 1:9 "If we confess our sins, He is faithful and just and will forgive our sins and cleanse us from all unrighteousness." Confession is more than just saying I confess my sin and I am sorry I sinned. Confessing is agreeing with God about your sin and that you personally sinned against Him, and that you intend to change those sinful things.

As I pondered my situation, I could hear my friend Bobbie speaking in my ear, saying, "trials reveal what we really believe and what is really inside our hearts. They test us. And until we are in a situation where we have no choice but to face an issue, we need to deal with it."

My rebellious spirit, my pride, my shame, my feelings of low self-esteem and guilt, and the fact that I had allowed Satan's lies to separate me from God's love led me to lay them all on the altar before the Lord. Shame and guilt had kept me from accepting my true position as a child of God. Shame made me believe God would never speak to me again.

And so, one day, I began to pray to God about my situation. I listened for the voice of God, so I called my new friend and said to him, "I am a woman of God and if this relationship is to continue, we must make it permanent. I will not continue in this relationship as it is today." He came over, we sat and talked about what I was feeling, and as it turned out, he was feeling the exact way. We both went before God and asked for His forgiveness, and a few months later, we got married.

It is imperative that you fight against shame with confession, inner healing, and the truth of God's word. Saturate your life with scriptures. Encourage yourself! Standing on the truth of scriptures is the key. Because John 10:27-29 tells us that, "My sheep hear my voice; and I know them, and they follow me. I give them eternal life, and they will never perish, and no one will snatch them out of my hand. My father, who has given them to me, is greater than all, and no one is able to snatch them out of the father's hand."

We need to be in God's word regularly to know Him and what His word says. If I had not taken a stand with this relationship, and if I had not known and focused on what God's word says, we would have continued in sin. I am grateful for the Word of God and its guidance that says, His word is, "A lamp for my feet, a light on my path." When you feel that God is no longer listening to you, be patience, be expectant, and let go of worry and lack of control. Remind yourself of His faithfulness. Turn over your uncertainty to the one who is all-knowing and is the only one who will and can give you guidance and peace.

Remember nothing is too big for Him. He is the one who is large and in charge. And all He asks us to do is to believe and walk in faith. Remember, He is God, and you are not. He is aware of all your needs and can handle any situation you may have. All He asks is that we, "Walk by faith and not by sight."

In 2015, my friend Bobbie went home to be with the Lord, so today when I am facing a situation, I always remember her. I ask myself, *what would she say?* And Proverb 3:5-6 always comes to mind: "Trust in the Lord with all your heart and lean not to your own understanding; in all your ways submit to Him, and He will make your path straight."

# NOTE TO SELF
## HINDERANCES TO HEARING GOD'S VOICE

_____

_____

_____

_____

_____

_____

_____

_____

_____

_____

_____

_____

_____

_____

_____

_____

_____

_____

_____

_____

_____

_____

_____

_____

_____

_____

_____

# NOTE TO SELF
## HINDERANCES TO HEARING GOD'S VOICE

_____

_____

_____

_____

_____

_____

_____

_____

_____

_____

_____

_____

_____

_____

_____

_____

_____

_____

_____

_____

# CHAPTER 6

# STEPS TO GAIN THE ABILITY TO TRUST GOD WHEN LIFE IS HARD

"I CAN DO ALL THINGS THROUGH CHRIST
WHO STRENGTHENS ME."
PHILIPPIANS 4:13 (NIV)

**When things get hard, let go of thinking life should always go your way.** God answers every prayer, but He does not always answer, "Yes." Sometimes He says, "No" or "Wait."

We have free will to choose to do either good or bad, and so does everyone else in this world. So sometimes, terrible things happen. Sometimes, we do not get what we want because what we want would not be good for us. Remember that God knows more than you do. Remind yourself that God has your best interests in mind and loves you.

**Give up trying to be in control over your own destiny.** Put everything in God's hand. God is like a good parent—He does not give us what we want; He always gives us what we need.

**Ask God for help by praying on a regular basis.** Do not be afraid to let God know how you are feeling. You can tell God things that you cannot share with other people. However, remember that God never promised to shield you from difficulties. He only promised to be with you if you want Him to.

One thing I can tell you—getting angry and blaming other people will not help you get through your situation. I made that mistake and spent too many years in a bad place.

Blaming someone else did not aid in my healing until I started asking Him to be with me in my situation and change my heart. I was able to eventually move on from that place in my life.

When we put ourselves in God's healing hands, we may begin broken and damaged, but we end up whole and complete because God can help you endure more than you would ever be able to on your own. Scriptures tell us, in Isaiah 26:3, that, "Thou wilt keep Him in perfect peace whose mind is stayed on thee, because he trusts in thee." I found that when we experience trials or situations as we sometimes call them, they dig up the soil and let us see what we are made of.

One writer said, "A gem cannot be polished without friction, nor a man perfected without faith." Being on a spiritual path does not prevent us from facing dark times, but it teaches us how to use the darkness as a tool to grow. Situations or trials also train you. God must train His troops. God must prepare His children for the future. If it were not for the struggles, you would not have the strength to make it through. God is building you up even when it seems like He is breaking you. Sometimes God has to discipline everyone He loves.

**Take a deep breath and be grateful that you are alive.** Give gratitude for your life, your family, your physical well-being, whatever comes to mind. Make a list of things you appreciate about life. Even if it is as basic as a roof over your head or food on the table. Examine your life; I found that people who refuse to examine their lives are defensive, they rarely apologize, and they tend to isolate themselves from the input of others. People who refuse to live an examined life, arbitrarily choose from whom they will receive. I encourage you to read or listen to the stories of others; their experiences will help you. Someone said to me, "God doesn't keep us from tests and trials; He helps us get through them."

Also tell God you are thankful for them. The simple act of noticing the good things in your life helps you to have a more positive attitude and helps you see God's hand in all things good or bad.

**Consider your motives for wanting to hear from God.** Honestly reflect on why you want to hear from God. Is it because you are truly open to whatever God has to say, and are you committed to putting His guidance into action and fulfilling His purpose even when doing so is challenging? Or is it for a selfish reason, such as wanting to feel righteous or comforted? Repent for any wrong motives. Ask God to give you an openness to hear and respond faithfully to what He wants to tell you.

**Know that this too shall pass.** Nothing except Heaven is forever. Trust that God has not forgotten about you or is not listening. Although God may seem silent regarding your specific requests or petitions, remember He is always listening to you, waiting to respond at the proper time. You must trust and have faith in Him.

**Be careful of the advice you receive from others, and the noise of the world.** We all have been given the Spirit of God. Good friends can confirm and advise, but they can never replace the wisdom of the Holy Spirit. You must let go of the things of this world that seem more interesting than the things of God. Even though, when a crisis occurs, and you go to others first instead of God, you want their counsel, their opinion, and you want them to approach God and hear for you. When this happens, you insert someone else in the middle of your personal relationship with God. Just remember,

Jeremiah 33:3 tells us, "Call unto me, and I will answer thee, and shew three great and might things, which thou knowest not."

**Be Still.** Sometimes you need quietness; get away from all the distractions around you. Stop all you are doing and listen, concentrate, and focus on God. The Bible says when you pray, go to your room, and close the door. Pray privately to your Father who is with you. Your Father sees what you do in private. He will reward you.

Scriptures tell us in the Book of Psalms 46:10, "Be still and know that I am God." Be quiet, listen, concentrate, and focus on God. You will be surprised at what you hear.

"A JOURNEY TO THE UNKNOWN SHORES NEEDS
A PORT, A SHIP, A WIND; BUT MORE IMPORTANT
THAN ALL OF THEM: COURAGE; COURAGE TO
LEAVE THE KNOWN FOR THE UNKNOWN!"
MEHMET MURAT İIDAN

# NOTE TO SELF
## STEPS TO GAIN THE ABILITY TO TRUST
## GOD WHEN LIFE IS HARD

_____

_____

_____

_____

_____

_____

_____

_____

_____

_____

_____

_____

_____

_____

_____

_____

_____

_____

_____

_____

_____

_____

_____

_____

_____

# NOTE TO SELF
## STEPS TO GAIN THE ABILITY TO TRUST GOD WHEN LIFE IS HARD

_____
_____
_____
_____
_____
_____
_____
_____
_____
_____
_____
_____
_____
_____
_____
_____
_____
_____
_____
_____
_____
_____
_____
_____
_____

# CHAPTER 7

# NAVIGATING THE UNKNOWN WITH CONFIDENCE AND HOPE

"FOR GOD HAS NOT GIVEN US THE SPIRIT OF FEAR, BUT
OF POWER AND OF LOVE AND OF A SOUND MIND."
2 TIMOTHY 1:7 (KJV)

When you have navigated the unknown for so long and you have been beat down physically and mentally, it is hard to tell that your season of change has occurred. I had been gripped by fear of failure, fear of being laughed at, fear of not knowing enough or being good enough. I did not realize I was in a new season. God had brought me out of darkness into the marvelous light. One day I felt a call to take on this new challenge in the ministry. I could feel the Spirit drawing me into a new endeavor. I did not know what was going to happen. This was one time I wanted a peek into the future. I said Lord help me have confidence, trust, and faith in you for my life and for this new direction. I needed Him to help me put one foot in front of the other, to do the next thing, to continue walking in His way. Acts 20:22 says, "And now, compelled by the Spirit, I am going to Jerusalem, not knowing what will happen to me there."

During navigation, I had not realized that my life had changed to the point that I had become an ordained minister and had received a Doctorate in Theology. I thought, *Oh Lord during all my struggles something good has happen to me. Lord, I am in a new season of life and did not even know it or recognize things had changed.* Being in the company of other women of God, I came to realize that fear is a normal human emotion, and that others have had feelings of fear at some point in their lives.

I found that it is not a sin to feel fear and anxiety. I learned that there are ways to deal with these feelings when they occur, and to not allow myself to be crippled. Rather, I learned to tell God that I was fearful and why I was fearful. I would ask Him to help me get over the fear of stepping out in faith to become what He has called me to do and to be. I would rebuke the enemy by repeating a scripture, especially Psalm 56:3-4, that says, "What time I am afraid, I will trust in thee. In God I will praise His word, in God I have put my trust; I will not fear what flesh can do unto me."

I thought if I wait for fear to go away on its own, I will never start doing the things I was called to do. I found that if I walked in obedience to God's calling, the fear would dissipate. So, one day, I decided fear would not attack me and try to convince me that there is no solution to my circumstances. I refused to allow fear to convince me that there are no way things would work out, that things were never going to change.

2 Timothy 1:7 says," For God did not give us a spirit of fear, but a spirit of power, love and self-discipline."

So, I decided to be bold and diligent, knowing that God would be with me as I did my best. One day as I was studying the scriptures, I found in Philippian 1:6, "Being confident of this very thing, that He who begun a good work in you will perform it until the day of Christ

Jesus." When you enter a relationship with God and trust Him with all your concerns, you put aside those unhealthy beliefs that you have about yourself. Trusting God with my life has brought good results.

I realized at that moment, I had little to do with my achievement, I was just following God's lead. Especially because once I allowed God to take full control of my life, I experienced substantial changes.

Start encouraging yourself in the Lord. In the Book of Deuteronomy, the 28th Chapter, the Lord says, "And the Lord will make you the head and not the tail; you shall be above only, and not beneath, if you heed the commandments of the Lord your God". I started to personalize those scriptures and applied them to my situations. Find your confidence. Tell yourself, "I can do all things through Christ who gives me strength."

When I left the seminary, God allowed me to become part of a ministry for women. These women had all attended the seminary and I was looking for a platform to help other women and people in the community. Joining this group allowed me to develop confidence. I began to work in the community, feeding the homeless, participating in health fairs and youth projects, and organizing women conferences. This gave me an opportunity to meet other women in the ministry as well.

One thing I suggest is getting a mentor. I sought out someone, a woman of God, as a mentor and she taught me so much about being a woman in the ministry as well as about mentoring and witnessing to other in in need. Women who had gone through some of the same experiences I had. Watch for changes in your life. Sometimes our seasons are short and sometimes they are long. Regardless of their length, when we align ourselves with God, He takes us through, no matter the circumstances.

The plan that He says He has for us begins to unfold. One day I felt that one of the things I am most grateful for is my new husband.

He encourages me in the ministry. He is a true man of God. Without this constant encouragement, I do not know if I could fully embrace this new place, I am in. I know that giving my life to the Lord and trusting Him to navigate, whether it is in the dark or the light, is the best decision I have ever made.

I am working as hard as I can to meet my challenges. I want to do my best, knowing that the Lord is with me all the way. I know that all I have to do is be brave, fight fear, and anxiety, and just focus on God and the task ahead of me. I do not know how long this season is going to last; all I know is if I plant good seeds there will be a great harvest. I feel so hopeful about the future, not that I do not expect trials and tribulations, The fact that I have a relationship with the Lord, my soul is connected to Him, and that He will fight my battles, is all I need.

I encourage you, allow God to navigate for you, just follow His lead. He will never lead you wrong. He said in His word that, "He will never leave you nor forsake you." God's plan for you is of good and not of evil. "He will give you a future and a hope". I know you cannot see that right now, but trust Him with you soul, and one day you will soon see your season of darkness is now filled with light.

As you allow God to navigate your life, sit down and write a note to God. Explain what you want out of life. Tell Him what you want Him to do in your life. Make your wishes plain and watch God do the rest. Scriptures tell us, in the Book of Habakkuk 3:2, "Write down the vision and make it plain. For the vision is yet for the appointed time; it testifies about the end and will not lie. Though it delays, wait for it, since it will certainly come and not be late."

Just know life is not about getting rid of our burdens, it is about finding grace to carry them to the place He wants you to go.

Change is not easy, especially when it means a transition into difficulty or the unknown. Jesus was very well acquainted with seasons. His life and ministry varied through seasons and challenges. He experienced seasons of miracles and seasons of teachings. Seasons of favor, and seasons where He was abandoned by all but a few.

The Book of Ecclesiastes 3:1 says, "For everything there is a season, a time for every activity under heaven."

2 Chronicles 19:11 says, "Be bold and diligent. And God be with you as you do your best."

Hebrews 10:35 says, "Do not throw away your confidence, which has a great reward."

Let the Lord know that you are ready to listen to His voice, ask Him to be your gentle Shepherd, to lead you to where He wants you to go.

"TO KEEP FEAR IN ITS PLACE, WE NEED TO KNOW
WHAT IT IS AND WHAT ITS PLACE SHOULD BE."
DAVID JEREMIAH

# NOTE TO SELF
## NAVIGATING THE UNKNOWN WITH CONFIDENCE AND HOPE

_____
_____
_____
_____
_____
_____
_____
_____
_____
_____
_____
_____
_____
_____
_____
_____
_____
_____
_____
_____
_____

# Note to Self
## Navigating the Unknown with Confidence and Faith

_____

_____

_____

_____

_____

_____

_____

_____

_____

_____

_____

_____

_____

_____

_____

_____

_____

_____

_____

_____

_____

_____

_____

_____

_____

_____

_____

# CHAPTER 8

# Navigating Unfamiliar Paths

"Before I formed you in the womb, I knew you,
before you were born, I sanctified you; I
ordained you as a prophet to the nation."
Jeremiah 1:5 KJV)

Entering the unknown can release a world of possibilities. It allows us to minister to others who have been in a struggle for so long. Being comfortable with the discomfort of not knowing is not easy, but it calls on us to locate our inner compass and see the world without harm. It helps us to learn to trust God no matter how scary it gets.

I encourage you to use these tips to help you navigate through uncertain times:

- **Be committed to overcome, no matter your situation**. When commitment is present, we possess a sense of purpose that tells us why we are doing what we are doing. We are guided by a vision that provides passions and hope to our lives. Commitment gives us a reason to wake up each morning and meet life's challenges.

- **Be ready for a challenge**. We have all heard at some point, "It's not what happens to you, but what you do with what happens to you that matter." When faced with a problem the words that you speak about it and your ability to overcome it play crucial roles as to whether you adapt to it, or not. Being ready for a challenge is important because you will be more flexible and creative toward the circumstances, and more likely to learn from the situation instead of feeling hopeless and defeated.

- **Be in control**. Often, we feel a heightened sense of stress during periods of our life when we feel we have less personal control. Prolonged stress can increase our chances of experiencing mental and emotional problems. To achieve a sense of personal control is identifying what is and is not within your control or influence. Otherwise, you will remain shackled to patterns of thinking that will continue to fuel your emotions and your behavior that will sabotage your progress.

- **Obtain yourself an accountability partner.** This is someone who you can trust will hold what you have entrusted to them in confidence. Perhaps if you have a church sister to help pray you through that would be awesome. Keep in mind, a mentoring partner does not replace God; they point you toward God and help you remain connected to Him.

- **Establish a relationship with God**. He is a very present help in times of trouble. In Hebrews 13:5, the word of God says, "I will never leave thee, nor forsake thee."

- **Get spiritual support**. Always share what is going on in your life with your pastor if you have one.

- **Get a godly mentor if you can**. This person may serve as your accountability partner. They can help you in times of discouragement by giving you godly advice. This can help you avoid some mistakes.

- **Surround yourself with positive people.** These are people who are going to encourage you and can give you constructive advice. Be careful; people who are never able to give compliments or give you good advice, they will pull you down eventually, so be careful who you choose for this assignment.

- **Keep yourself motivated.** Joshua 1:9 says, "Be strong and of good courage. Do not be afraid; nor be dismayed, for the Lord your God is with you wherever you go." To help motivate yourself repeat Psalm 16:2, "The Lord is my rock, and my fortress, and my deliverer; my God, my strength in whom I will trust, my buckler, and the horn of my salvation, any my high tower."

- **Make time to pray daily so that you can stay strong.** The Bible tells us in 1 Thessalonians 5:17 to "pray without ceasing". When you pray, you will receive the wisdom of God, and you will receive peace. It is important to keep praying because the scripture says, in 2 Corinthians 4:8-9, that, "We are troubled on every side, yet not distressed; we are perplexed, but not in despair; persecuted, but not forsaken; cast down, but not destroyed."

- **Ask God to help you and to guide you.** When you stay connected to God, when you stay under His covering, you leave no room for deception, because subtle deceptions are on a rampage in the Kingdom of God. Ask others to pray with you and for you.

- **Saturate your life with scriptures.** Know some encouraging scriptures that you can repeat to yourself to strengthen you in times of discouragement. Post key verses around you. Post them on your phone, mirror, or computer. Proverb 3:5-6 is a good example as well as Isaiah 41:10; Psalm 23, Psalm 91, and Isaiah 43:2.

- **Start a journal.** Write down all the ways God has been faithful. Make a list of things that you would like to see happen in your life. Sometimes it seems as though our season of darkness is long. It is hard to see progress when we are feeling bad for extended periods of time. It is especially important to jot down things that we have put before God to see if He has answered our prayers. You will be surprised to see that He has answered, and you did not notice it.

- **Set aside time for yourself.** When we are constantly facing trials and tribulations, it is easy to feel anxious, including other unhealthy feelings. Having some alone time can help you think and make clear decisions. You can use this time to relax, meditate, read scriptures, or just curl up with a delightful book.

- **Walk by faith.** 2 Corinthians 5:7 tells you to, "Walk by faith not by sight." Also, Hebrews 11:6 says, "And without faith it is impossible to please God. Faith is the substance of things hope for, but the evidence of things not seen." Meditate, pray, read scriptures, but most of all put your trust in God. As you pray just know that God is working everything out for you. Release all control to God, and He will navigate you to the place where He wants you to be.

# NOTE TO SELF
## NAVIGATING UNFAMILIAR PATHS

# NOTE TO SELF
## NAVIGATING UNFAMILIAR PATHS

CHAPTER 9

# Your Testimony Can Bless the Life of Others

"For His anger lasts only a moment, but His
favor lasts a lifetime; weeping may remain for
a night but rejoicing comes in the morning."
Psalm 30:5 (NIV)

Everyone's testimony is powerful because it is a story about moving from death to life. Giving your personal testimony is a way of sharing the gospel with others, by explaining your personal experience. It gives others an example of how God changes lives. It shows that what you went through was not a waste. Your struggles, your situation, your circumstances were not for you; it was a class that you can teach others who are struggling. Regardless of who you have become, or what you used to be, regardless of your status, you have been taught survival skills that you can pass on to others.

Your testimony is proof that God is alive and actively involved in your life. Your testimony about how God showed mercy to you through Christ will bring His hope to others. You may not realize it, but you have been given firsthand knowledge of the goodness of God. The journey you had to take was for this purpose. Your experience can now be a lesson for others. You can say for sure that, "God will not leave you nor forsake you." You can say without reservation as given in James 1:2 "Count it all joy," because you know if we allow God to be in control, everything will work out for our good.

Your testimony will challenge and build others' faith to grow. You can tell others that when you did not know what to do during your circumstances, God knew what you needed before you asked. Think about it, every time we hear that someone is freed from the grip of sin and the devil, the more we should praise God for their salvation. Because now you know for sure that God can do "exceedingly abundantly, beyond anything that you could think or ask of Him" (Ephesian 3:20).

Romans 8:31 says, "What, then shall we say to these things? If God is for us, who can be against us?" Your story is unique even if you do not think so. At some point, you realized that life was not working out so well when you were running it on your own and that you needed help.

Your testimony may be extreme and radical, or it might be calm and professional. Nevertheless, testimonies usually show God's love and mercy because Romans 3:23 says, "For all have sinned and fall short of the glory of God."

In sharing your testimony do not be ashamed of what God has done in your life. Do not be afraid of telling people that God saved you from sin and shame. God is faithful. If you confess your sins, He will forgive your sins. He will forgive every wrong thing you have done. He will make you pure. I encourage you to boast about God's mighty power. Soon others will feel that if God did it for you, then He can and will do it for them if they turn over their lives to Him. Philippians 3:13 tells us, "I have not achieved it, but I focus on this one thing: Forgetting the past and looking forward to what lies ahead."

Encourage others to keep praying and keep reading the word of God. Others will learn that during your trials and tribulations, God did not leave your side. He did not leave you alone in your tribulations. They will learn that prayer aligns them with God's will. Accept Christ as the Lord of your life, and if someone asks about your hope as a believer, always be ready to explain about it in a quiet, gentle, and respectful way.

Also, in sharing your testimony, it removes your own fear and gives you courage. In speaking about what God has done in your life, it helps you remember the goodness of God. When you recount what God has done in the past, it gives you even more faith and courage for living in the present. Sharing your testimony can become a resource for other people. Sharing how God worked in your past helps you encourage others who may be going through some similar situation. They will see in you the hope they long to have. Your testimony can become the key to help someone else unlock their own prison.

God's word tells us to share our hope as a believer. 1 Peter 3:15-16 says, "But in your hearts revere Christ as Lord. Always be prepared to give an answer to everyone who asks you to give the reason for the hope that you have. But do this with gentleness and respect, keeping a clear conscience, so that those who speak maliciously against your good behavior in Christ may be ashamed of their slander."

Be ready to tell your truth with faith and confidence. As you look back over the lives of women from the Bible, it should give you hope because their story blesses our lives today. Their story teaches us to praise His might, trust His power, focus on His love, Pray His will and follow His light and rejoice.

Mary, Elizabeth, Sarah, and Hannah navigated the unknown. Mary was visited by an angel. He said she would bare a Son and call his name Jesus. All this despite her relationship with Joseph. God used her to accomplish His purpose. She was able to navigate a road that she knew nothing about. Elizabeth, the Mother of John, was barren. However, the Lord blessed her, and she gave birth to John the Baptist. Sarah, Abraham's wife, was barren. The Lord visited Sarah as He had spoken. At the set time of which He had spoken, she conceived and bore a son, Isaac, even in her old age. Not only that, but she also became the Mother of Nations.

Hannah was barren and had a bitter soul. She prayed to the Lord as she wept in anguish for a male child and vowed to give him back to Him all the days of his life. She conceived and bore a son, Samuel. The Lord heard her prayers and she bore three sons and two daughters. For with God nothing is impossible. We must be obedient and listen to the voice of God and be ready to step out in faith and trust Him to lead the way. The story of these women still testifies today about the goodness of our Lord and Savior, and how He moved in their lives.

Therefore, your testimony should always be, if He did it for them, if He did it for me, He can do it for you.

"IF A PERSON FIRMLY BELIEVE THAT GOD IS ALWAYS
WITH HIM, THEN EVEN IF HE IS THROWN INTO THE
DEPTHS OF THE SEA, HE WILL BE PRESERVED IN BODY
AND SOUL, AND WILL ENJOY GREATER SOLACE AND
COMFORT THAN ALL THIS WORLD CAN OFFER."
JULIAN OF NORWICH—FAMOUS INSPIRATIONAL QUOTES

# NOTE TO SELF
## YOUR TESTIMONY CAN BLESS THE LIFE OF OTHERS

_____

_____

_____

_____

_____

_____

_____

_____

_____

_____

_____

_____

_____

_____

_____

_____

_____

_____

_____

_____

_____

_____

# NOTE TO SELF
## YOUR TESTIMONY CAN BLESS THE LIFE OF OTHERS

_____
_____
_____
_____
_____
_____
_____
_____
_____
_____
_____
_____
_____
_____
_____
_____
_____
_____
_____
_____
_____
_____
_____
_____
_____
_____
_____
_____

# CHAPTER 10

# YOUR BELIEF DURING UNKNOWN TIMES

"GOD IS NOT A MAN, THAT HE SHOULD LIE; NEITHER
THE SON OF MAN, THAT HE SHOULD REPENT: HATH
HE SAID, AND SHALL HE NOT DO IT? OR HATH HE
SPOKEN, AND SHALL HE NOT MAKE IT GOOD?"
NUMBER 23:19 (KJV)

**God will provide for you.** Philippians 4:19 says, "But my God will supply all your needs according to His riches in glory by Christ Jesus." Psalm 37:25 says, "I was young and now I am old, yet I have never seen the righteous forsaken or their seed begging bread."

**God will protect you.** Psalm 91 says, "He that dwelleth in the secret place of the most-high shall abide under the shadow of the almighty."

**God will lead you.** 2 Timothy 2:15 says, "The steps of a good man are ordered by the Lord."

**God hears you.** Psalm 34:17 tells us, "The righteous cry, and the Lord heareth, and delivereth them out of all their troubles."

**God will forgive you.** 1 John 1:9 tells us, "If we confess our sins, He is faithful and just and will forgive us our sins and purify us from all unrighteousness."

**God loves you.** He loves you because He chose to. He is full of grace and mercy." Psalm 23:6 says, "Surely goodness and mercy shall follow me all the days of my life: and I will dwell in the house of the Lord forever."

John 3:16 says, "For this is how God so loved the world: He gave His one and only Son, so that everyone who believes in Him will not perish but have eternal life."

"HE, JESUS, DID NOT SAY, YOU WILL NEVER HAVE A ROUGH PASSAGE, YOU WILL NEVER BE OVER-STRAINED, YOU WILL NEVER FEEL UNCOMFORTABLE, BUT HE DID SAY, "YOU WILL NEVER BE OVERCOME." JULIAN OF NORWICH—FAMOUS INSPIRATIONAL QUOTES

# NOTE TO SELF
## YOUR BELIEF DURING UNKNOWN TIMES

_____

_____

_____

_____

_____

_____

_____

_____

_____

_____

_____

_____

_____

_____

_____

_____

_____

_____

_____

_____

_____

# NOTE TO SELF
## YOUR BELIEF DURING UNKNOWN TIMES

_____

_____

_____

_____

_____

_____

_____

_____

_____

_____

_____

_____

_____

_____

_____

_____

_____

_____

_____

_____

_____

_____

_____

_____

_____

_____

_____

_____

_____

CHAPTER 11

# EXPECTATIONS WHEN NAVIGATING THE UNKNOWN

"NOW TO HIM WHO IS ABLE TO DO EXCEEDING,
ABUNDANTLY ABOVE ALL THAT WE ASK OR THINK,
ACCORDING TO THE POWER THAT WORKETH IN US."
EPHESIANS 3:20 (KIV)

- **God has a blessing waiting for you.** Trust Him, step out, and choose obedience. Abraham and Sarah are a good example of a couple who navigated the unknown. They trusted God and He kept His end of the deal. He gave them a son, Isaac.
- **Even with a clear destination in my mind, the path can be fuzzy and unknown.** Keep striving for a better day.
- **Its ok to take a wrong turn.** But once you recognize your mistake, stop and ask God for guidance to help you get to where you want to go. He is there to help you get back on track. Psalm 37:23 says, "The step of a good man is ordered by the Lord: and He delighteth in His way." He will be your GPS.

- **Even though, God's way of navigating is strange, follow Him.** He knows the experiences that will prepare you best for what is ahead of you. He is familiar with all the obstacles, twists, and turns.
- **God wants the best for you.** Even when it does not seem like it in the moment, it is in these time that you must trust Him to navigate you to where you need to be.
- **You are not weak; you are strong.** The devil delights in making us think we are weak and incapable, but the truth is that we have all of God's strength available to us when we lean on and rely on Him.
- **God knows where you are.** He has not forgotten you. He wants you to know how much He loves you. He wants a deeper friendship with you. He wants to take you on a journey of a lifetime.

When you are navigating the unknown, you must expect that comfort comes to God's people in their times of need; your strength and your weakness are in the hands of the Lord. Because of His love, He will preserve your strength and help you in your weakness, because God's love is the one thing that unites all human existence. And because love can inspire, encourage, and lighten our hearts.

Psalm 73:25-26 tells us, "Whom have I in heaven but You? I want nothing more on earth, but You. My body and my heart may grow weak, but God is the strength of my heart and all I need forever." Revelation 21:3-4 says, "God Himself will be with them and be their God. He will wipe every tear from their eyes. There will be no more death or mourning or crying or pain, for the old order of things has passed away."

"NO MATTER WHAT YOU WANT, YOU HAVE AN
INVISIBLE SUPPORT SYSTEM THAT IS ALL READY TO
HELP YOU GET IT. YOU DON'T HAVE TO UNDERSTAND
HOW IT WORKS, JUST KNOW THAT IT DOES."
AUTHOR UNKNOWN

# NOTE TO SELF
## EXPECTATIONS WHEN NAVIGATING THE UNKNOWN

_____

_____

_____

_____

_____

_____

_____

_____

_____

_____

_____

_____

_____

_____

_____

_____

_____

_____

_____

_____

_____

_____

"THE YEARS OF OUR LIFE ARE SEVENTY, OR EVEN BY REASON OF
STRENGTH EIGHTY;  YET, THEIR SPAN IS BUT TOIL AND TROUBLE;
THEY ARE SOON GONE, AND WE FLY AWAY. SO, TEACH US TO
NUMBER OUR DAYS THAT WE MAY GET A HEART OF WISDOM."
PSALM 90:10, 12

# NOTE TO SELF
## EXPECTATIONS WHEN NAVIGATING THE UNKNOWN

_____

_____

_____

_____

_____

_____

_____

_____

_____

_____

_____

_____

_____

_____

_____

_____

_____

_____

_____

_____

_____

_____

_____

CHAPTER 12

# ROADBLOCKS TO HEALING

"AND IT WILL BE SAID: BUILD UP, BUILD UP,
PREPARE THE ROAD! REMOVE THE OBSTACLES
OUT OF THE WAY OF MY PEOPLE."
ISAIAH 57:14 (NIV)

- **Ignoring your problems.** Ignoring a problem never makes it go away. It just keeps hurting us until we let God help us dig it up and deal with it. You can avoid dealing with the root of your problem, but they always resurface, and make you unhappy.
- **Unwillingness to face reality.** You should not let your past become an excuse to stay the way you are. If you have been running from your past and you desire to be whole, it is time to learn how to communicate with yourself and stop blaming your past failures for staying where you are. Facing the past does not mean that you are not to focus on it but focusing too much on the past can be destructive. God wants you to face it and move on.
- **Blaming others.** Blaming others for your misery and problems will always prevent you from moving on with

your life. Blaming is a way for you to continue to run away from reality, because if you blame someone else, you will never break free and take ownership for your own behavior.

- **Self-Pity.** Self-pity never helps you recover. Self-pity comes from an unwillingness to accept a situation or circumstance in your life. Self-pity drains you of energy and leaves you feeling hopeless and sometimes depressed. Rather, self-pity is an enemy and should be treated as such. Self-pity brags about how bad you have it in life.

- The devil delights in making you think you are weak and incapable of change, but the truth is that you have all of God's strength available to you when you lean on and rely on Him. 1 John 4:4 tells us that, "Greater is He that is in you, than He who is in the world." You are indeed weak and incapable in many ways, but God, who is the greater one, lives in you. You got what it takes to do what you need to do!

- **Lack of fellowship with Jesus.** To be free from sin, you must receive Him as your Lord and Savior. To be healed and live in health, it is necessary to receive Him as your great doctor and believe He bore your sickness in pain. We are invited to have fellowship with Jesus through His Spirit. When He went away, He told His disciples that He would send them another comforter to be in close fellowship with them. You do not ever need to feel that Jesus is far away because He is as close as your breath or heartbeat. He is in you. He wants to have a close, personal relationship with you. When you accept Christ as your Savior, He does an amazing work in you. He comes to live inside of you and gives you a new nature and a new spirit, both of which are His.

- John 14:20 says, "On that day you will realize that I am in my father, and you are in me, and I am in you." John 1:12 (KJV) says, "But as many as received Him, to them gave he power to become the sons of God, even to them that believe on His name."

- **Unbelief and doubt.** Unbelief and doubt can stop your progress. You must believe in yourself and in God to move to another level. Not believing in yourself and God will kill your dreams or vision faster than you know. Belief is the cornerstone to every successful person's vision and dreams.

- When you do not believe in yourself, other people notice it. You begin to attract more of the energy you put out, so you do not want to be putting out a lot of self-doubt and negative vibes. Take the time to reflect on the roadblocks to healing. Remind yourself of your past victories and the positive impact your life has had on the lives of others. If you want others to value your contributions, you must value them first.

"NO MATTER HOW WOUNDED WE ARE WHEN WE BEGIN OUR JOURNEY TOWARD WHOLENESS, GOD HAS GUARANTEED OUR SUCCESS AS LONG AS WE DON'T GIVE UP."
JOYCE MEYER

# Note to Self
## Roadblocks to Healing

_____

_____

_____

_____

_____

_____

_____

_____

_____

_____

_____

_____

_____

_____

_____

_____

_____

_____

_____

_____

_____

_____

_____

# NOTE TO SELF
## ROADBLOCKS TO HEALING

_____
_____
_____
_____
_____
_____
_____
_____
_____
_____
_____
_____
_____
_____
_____
_____
_____
_____
_____
_____
_____
_____
_____
_____
_____

CHAPTER 13

# BREAKING THE TORMENT OF FEAR, GUILT, AND SHAME

"THEREFORE, THERE IS NOW NO CONDEMNATION
FOR THOSE WHO ARE IN CHRIST JESUS."
ROMANS 8:1 (NIV)

One of the most common ways in which Satan attacks people is by making them relive their past mistakes. One of the heaviest burdens you can carry is guilt. Most of us who know the weight of guilt and shame is because of something we have done and at other times it is because something others have done to us. But the biggest lie we often tell ourselves is that shame and guilt are a form of punishment from God. We feel that He wants us to carry the burden of guilt as a form of penance because we have been bad.

Kristalyn Salters-Pedneault, PhD, from Verywell Mind, says "Understanding shame and guilt can be important for your health. Shame is a powerful emotion that can cause people to feel defective, unacceptable, even damaged beyond repair. We can sometimes confuse shame with guilt, a related but different emotion, because guilt is a feeling you get when you did something wrong, or perceived you did something wrong. And shame is a feeling that your whole self is wrong, and it may not be related to a specific behavior or event. "When you feel guilty about the wrong thing you did, you can take steps to make up for it and put it behind you. But feeling shame or being convinced that you are the thing that is wrong, offers no clear-cut way to 'come back' to feeling more positive about yourself. Therefore, that's the difference between shame and guilt."

Isaiah 54:4 tells us, "Fear not, for you shall not be ashamed; neither be confounded and depressed, for you shall not be put to shame. For you shall forget the shame of your youth, and you shall not remember the reproach of your widowhood anymore." Satan paints God in such a picture as if He is a ruthless judge who is not finished with you and your past. He wants you to think that you are worthless, and you can never succeed. He will recruit you to be his co-prosecutor against your own soul. He will tell you that you should never forgive those who have wronged you, but Matthew 6:14-15 says, "For if you forgive other people when they sin against you, your heavenly Father will also forgive you. But if you do not forgive others their sins, your father will not forgive your sins."

Fear, guilt, and shame are three of the most tormenting, destructive, and debilitating things that wounded people experience. But God promises us deliverance and freedom from them because fear, guilt, and shame are a burden. The devil will place his lies in your mind and make you believe your past. He continually reminds you of your failures to keep you stuck. He wants you to think that what happened in the past was your fault. He lies about his power and make you feel you are powerless. He whispers lies in your ear such as:

- If you were a better wife or husband, you would not have been abused.

- If you were stronger, you would not have been sexually attacked or beaten.
- You are a coward; you never stand up for yourself.
- If you were smarter, you would not be rejected.
- You are not pretty enough.
- You are too fat; no one wants you.
- You messed up. You let people down.

Understand that people do not abuse you, misuse you, or mistreat you because there is something wrong with you. It is because there is something wrong with them. People who are broken and wounded always hurt others. Most often, people cannot recover until they unload their guilt and shame, they carry around with them every day. When it comes to our emotions, guilt has a lot of power. Guilt can help you acknowledge your actions and fuels your motivation to improve your behavior. Guilt can also lead you to become preoccupied about what you could have done differently. Guilt can linger and hold you back long after others have forgotten or forgiven what happened. This is not how you want to live, and you do not want to be one of those people who hurt others. Talk to your pastor or seek out a therapist to help you figure out how to get rid of unhealthy behaviors. Keep focus on why you want to change so that you can live confidently for Him because the grace of our Lord Jesus Christ is with us.

"WHAT YOU BELIEVE ABOUT YOURSELF IS MORE
IMPORTANT THAN WHAT ANYONE ELSE BELIEVE."
JOYCE MEYER

God does not want you to feel guilt, or shame, because your actual guilt before God is what Jesus took upon Himself to the cross. 1 Timothy 2:6 says, "He gave His life to purchase freedom for everyone.

This is the message God gave the world at just the right time." Therefore, on the deepest level, you are no longer guilty before God. Your ransom has been paid, your sins forgiven, your guilt removed, and your life restored. Psalm 49:7-8, says, "Truly no man can ransom another, or give to God the price of his life, for the ransom of their life is costly and can never suffice."

Shame tells us we are not worthy of God's grace, so we can believe that we are not able to approach God as our Father. This can come about from abusive examples of God, by being condemned by our consciences, or through the lies of Satan. So, you no longer need to believe the lie that the guilt and shame you are experiencing are a form of punishment from God. Instead, the fear, shame, and guilt you experience are a natural consequence for doing something you should not have done. As a reminder, you are not perfect but have a perfect Savior who was punished for your sins but is there to give you the power to overcome, grow, and change.

Romans 8:1 tell us, "There is therefore now no condemnation for those who are in Christ Jesus." Not only has our slate been wiped cleaned, but it remains clean all because of the beautiful and underserved sacrifice of Jesus. Repenting and getting past the guilt, blame, and shame are important to Jesus. It is important because Jesus wants us to turn from the things that are ruling and governing our lives.

Micah 7:19 says, "You will again have compassion on us; you will tread our sins under foot and hurl all our iniquities into the depth of the sea."

1 Peter 1:6-7 says, "For a little while you may have had to suffer grief in all kinds of trials. These have come so that your faith may be proven genuine and may result in praise, glory, and honor when Jesus Christ is revealed."

# NOTE TO SELF
## BREAKING THE TORMENT OF FEAR, GUILT, AND SHAME

# NOTE TO SELF
## BREAKING THE TORMENT OF FEAR, GUILT, AND SHAME

## CHAPTER 14

# GOD GIVES US PURPOSE AND POWER TO NAVIGATE THE UNKNOWN

"I CAN DO EVERYTHING THROUGH HIM
WHO GIVES ME STRENGTH."
PHILIPPIANS 4:13 (NIV)

When you sit with the word of God, you should pray and ask God for wisdom because the Holy Spirit is your teacher. Therefore, you can ask Him to illuminate the word and give you some insight. Sometimes, we often feel lost and do not know which way to turn during these unknown times. By asking for wisdom and instruction, we can be led by the Holy Spirit to the place and the plan that the Lord has for us. During our payer times, we pray for strength and insight to make it from one day to the next. His word tells us in Philippians 4:19, "But my God shall supply all your needs according to His riches in glory by Christ Jesus." Also, He tells us in Philippians 4:6, "Be careful for nothing; but in everything by prayer and supplication with thanksgiving let your request be made known unto God."

Prayer is important because when you are navigating the unknown, you do not know where you are headed, but the scriptures tell us, in Proverb 16:9, that, "In their hearts humans plan their course, but the Lord establishes their steps." If you understood where you were going, you would avoid the mud, the muck, the water, and the holes. Therefore, on your own, you would avoid certain places.

Not understanding that all the things and places that you would have avoided were part of the process for God to bring you to where He needs you to be. You see, during the unknown, you start to feel bogged down, and discouraged, and start to feel like your life it is out of control.

So, you may not be able to see the outcome of God's purpose for your life ten years into the future or even one day ahead. Yet, if you are living in God's plan, you do not need to worry or feel anxious about anything. The purpose will unfold all on its own. All you need to do is sit back, pray for God's guidance, and you will be pleasantly surprised at what God has in store for you. I have a question for you: If someone asked you do you know where you are headed, would you tell them? "Wherever God leads me"? If that is your answer, you are walking in the will of God, trusting, and believing that wherever you are headed, you are not alone.

As you navigate the unknown, I encourage you to be like Apostle Paul. He said in 1 Corinthians 11:1, "Follow my example, as I follow the example of Christ." In other words, live your life as Christ lived. God has special plans for you, if you will seek to become who He created you to be. He has given you your personality and gifts for a special reason. Ephesian 2:10 tells us that, "For we are God's handiwork created in Christ Jesus to do good works, which prepared in advance for us to do." You have been created purposefully by God. Only when you fully understand this concept will you see how important it is for your well-being that you discover God's intent for your life. Always remember that God made you unique because of the purpose He has in mind for you. He did not intend for you to feel lost or for you to worry about anything.

He did not intend for you to feel bogged down or feel that your life is out of control, especially because He said in Matthew 11:29, "Take my yoke upon you and learn from me, for I am gently and humble in heart, and you will find rest for your soul." Meditate on God's word because God is a God of purpose. 2 Timothy 1:9 says, "God has saved us and called us to a holy life, not because of anything we have done but because of His own purpose and grace, this grace was given us in Christ Jesus before the beginning of time."

" Psalm 33:11 says, "The plans of the Lord stand firm forever, the purposes of His heart through all generations." God is purposeful, and He will always carry out His purposes.

Isaiah 14:24 says, "The Lord Almighty has sworn, Surely, as I have planned, so it will be, and as I have purposed, so it will happen." You can be assured that God will fulfill His purpose for you as you allow Christ the Redeemer to restore you to Him and to the purposes, He has for you.

"PLAN ON AN AMAZING LIFE IN WHICH
YOU DO AMAZING THINGS."
JOYCE MEYER

Prayer:

Dear Father, you are the Creator, the Maker of all things, including me. I know that you have a purpose for my creation beyond anything I can understand. Help me to always keep my eyes upon you and your word as you reveal my purpose and your will. In Jesus' name, Amen.

# NOTE TO SELF
## GOD GIVES US PURPOSE AND POWER
## TO NAVIGATE THE UNKNOWN

# NOTE TO SELF
## GOD GIVES US PURPOSE AND POWER
## TO NAVIGATE THE UNKNOWN

_____

_____

_____

_____

_____

_____

_____

_____

_____

_____

_____

_____

_____

_____

_____

_____

_____

_____

_____

_____

_____

_____

_____

_____

CHAPTER 15

# TO DISCOVER YOUR PURPOSE, NEVER ASK THE CREATION, ASK THE CREATOR

"YET LORD, YOU ARE OUR FATHER; WE ARE
THE CLAY, AND YOU ARE THE POTTER;
WE ARE ALL THE WORK OF YOUR HAND."
ISAIAH 64:8 (HCSB)

Many people do not think that they have any worth or purpose. Yet the word of God, says in, Genesis 1:31 that, "God saw all that He had made, and it was good." There is something good in everything that God created. No matter how confused it looks to us, there is something good about every person, even though it may be hard to find it." We need to go to Him in prayer to find the good purpose for which He has made us. Philippians 2:13 says, "For it is God who worketh in you to will and to do of His good pleasures."

We have seen that no one knows a product and how it should work better than the one who made it or created it. In the same way, the one who created the product is the best one to fix it when it has become broken. When a potter makes a pot and sees that it has a flaw, the potter remolds the clay and starts over, or if the pot already has been fired in an oven, the potter smashes it and starts over again. As it is with you, when God created you, He knew exactly what purpose and plan He had for your life. And when you felt lost and broken, He came to your rescue. He gave you strength, and sometimes, He made you over. When you made mistakes and got out of His will, He allowed you to go through the mud and the water, among other things, to bring you back to your purpose in life. He allowed all of that to put you back in His will.

Sometimes the creation might not think it has any worth, but the Creator knows what it is made of, and what it needs to be put back together. God our Creator knows everything about us and what we need and when we need it. Knowing your purpose helps you achieve joy and happiness. It keeps you from feeling something is missing from your life. We are all born with the natural nature to believe in God and worship Him. The Creator wants each one of us to continue in the same state of obedience as we are born.

Psalm 139:7-12 (NIV) says, "Where can I go from your Spirit? Where can I flee from your presence? If I go up to the heavens, you are there; if I make my bed in the depth, you are there. If I rise on the wings of the dawn, If I settle on the far side of the sea, even there your hand will guide me, your right hand will hold me fast. If I say, "Surely the darkness will hide me and the light become night around me, even the darkness will not be dark to you; the night will shine like the day, for darkness is a light to you."

Some religions teach that the purpose of all of creation, including humanity, is to worship God alone and earn His pleasure. In life we are conflicted with all types of choices, both good and bad. The Creator wants us to make the right choices that would be pleasing to Him. Through the worship of God, you fulfill your life's purpose. By obeying, following, and praising Him, you will earn His pleasure and His favor.

At the same time, you will begin to value and realize the importance of your short time in this world and your purpose for being here.

God created you and made this world for you. You are getting benefits from all His creations. Realizing your life has meaning, your relationship with the Creator strengthens you and brings peace and tranquility into your life. Therefore, you are better able to handle what comes your way. Recognize and start living out your purpose to see how life-changing it can be.

"IT IS LOGICAL THAT IF YOU WALK WITHOUT PURPOSE IN THIS SHORT LIFE, YOU WILL END UP NOBODY. IT IS FAIR TO SAY ONE SHOULD DISCOVER ITS UNIQUE PURPOSE AND BE ENTWINED WITH IT. MANY PEOPLE DIE WITHOUT DISCOVERING THEIR TRUE PURPOSE, WITHOUT DOING ANYTHING OF VALUE WITH IT. 'THE RICHEST PLACE IN THE WORLD IS NOT THE MINES OF SOUTH AFRICA', 'IT IS, IN FACT, THE CEMETERY. BECAUSE IT IS A PLACE FILLED WITH THE DEAD WHO LEFT WITH UNTAPPED DREAMS, UNWRITTEN BOOKS, AND UNFINISHED BEGINNINGS. THE PURPOSE IS THE ORIGINAL INTENT FOR THE CREATION OF A THING, THAT IS IN THE MIND OF THE CREATOR OF THE THING. NOTHING IN LIFE IS WITHOUT PURPOSE."
DR. MYLES MUNROE

Once you discover your purpose, you will wake up every morning *excited*. The moment your feet hit the ground; you *cannot wait* to make a difference in the life of someone else. You will be excited to solve a problem, put a smile on someone's face, identify a solution to a problem, and you will go to bed at night with the satisfaction that you were your productive self.

You will ask yourself: *How can I use my purpose to make a difference?* I encourage you to continue to ask God, because He tells us in Matthew 7: 7-8, "To keep on asking, and you will receive what you ask for. Keep on seeking, and you will find. Keep on knocking, and the door will be opened to you. For everyone who asks, receives. Everyone who seeks, finds. And to everyone who knocks, the door will be opened."

Keep actively looking for answers to how you can use your purpose each day. Look for the path that you are supposed to take. Do your research. Understand that you may have to follow a lot of trails, some of which will take you to a dead end. That is OK; it is all part of the process. The path to living out your purpose is not always obvious or clear-cut. Take time and read every book you can get your hands on. Seek guidance and instruction from people who can help you live your purpose. Once you have opened your mind and heart to the possibilities of the universe, pay close attention to the people who show up. They are there to either teach you a lesson, challenge you, or help you along the path you are traveling.

The Bible says keep knocking. When you come upon a door of opportunity that you naturally believe is for you, you must knock. If you want to find out what is on the other side of the door, you must push it open and step through. Every day take a small step that will moves you in the direction of your purpose. Journal, write down your goal, then break it down into goals, and then even further into small, actionable steps. I promise you; these will add up quickly.

Believe within your spirit that this is why you are here. Make the decisions and choices that bring into your life the things that will help you fulfill your purpose. There will be times when you lose your footing or take a wrong step, even become discouraged, and that is OK. Each step, whether right or wrong, will teach you something and lead you closer to your purpose. Listen and pay attention to each one. Years from now, your life will be completely transformed because you will be living your purpose.

1 Peter 2:9 says, "But you are not like that, for you are a chosen people. You are royal priests, a holy nation, God very own possession. As a result, you can show others the goodness of God, for He called you out of darkness into His wonderful light." Luke 22:42 says, "Father, if thou be willing, remove this cup from me: nevertheless, not my will, but thine, be done". Say to yourself daily, I will yield to God's call on my life and submit myself to Him, I will humble myself so I can submit myself to the Lord and His will. I will submit to the Lord by giving my life to Him and being a sacrifice, by working in the kingdom for His glory, by serving His people, by spending time in His Word and in prayer."

Prayer:
Father, your word tells us in James 4:7 to "Submit yourself to God. Resist the devil, and he will flee from you." I repent for any kind of rebellion. Help me to recognize areas of rebellion in my life. I submit to your authority in my life because you are my Lord and my Savior. Let your peace reign in my life forever more and help me find my purpose. Amen.

---

LIFE IS LIKE RIDING A BICYCLE. TO KEEP YOUR
BALANCE, YOU MUST KEEP MOVING."
ALBERT EINSTEIN

# NOTE TO SELF
## TO DISCOVER YOUR PURPOSE, NEVER ASK THE CREATION, ASK THE CREATOR

_____

_____

_____

_____

_____

_____

_____

_____

_____

_____

_____

_____

_____

_____

_____

_____

_____

_____

_____

_____

_____

_____

"UNLESS YOU TRY TO DO SOMETHING BEYOND WHAT YOU HAVE ALREADY MASTERED, YOU WILL NEVER GROW."
RALPH WALDO EMERSON—FAMOUS INSPIRATIONAL QUOTES

NOTE TO SELF
TO DISCOVER YOUR PURPOSE, NEVER ASK
THE CREATION, ASK THE CREATOR

_____
_____
_____
_____
_____
_____
_____
_____
_____
_____
_____
_____
_____
_____
_____
_____
_____
_____
_____
_____

"YOU'RE NOT DEFINED BY YOUR PAST;  YOU'RE
PREPARED BY IT, YOU'RE STRONGER, MORE EXPERIENCED,
AND YOU HAVE GREATER CONFIDENCE."
JOEL OSTEEN—FAMOUS INSPIRATIONAL QUOTES

NOTE TO SELF
TO DISCOVER YOUR PURPOSE, NEVER ASK
THE CREATION, ASK THE CREATOR

_____

_____

_____

_____

_____

_____

_____

_____

_____

_____

_____

_____

_____

_____

_____

_____

_____

_____

"IN A LONG RUN, THE SHARPEST WEAPON OF
ALL IS A KIND AND GENTLE SPIRIT."
ANNE FRANK—FAMOUS INSPIRATIONAL QUOTES

NOTE TO SELF
TO DISCOVER YOUR PURPOSE, NEVER ASK
THE CREATION, ASK THE CREATOR

_____
_____
_____
_____
_____
_____
_____
_____
_____
_____
_____
_____
_____
_____
_____
_____
_____
_____
_____
_____
_____

"NOW I LOOK BEYOND WHAT I CAN'T DO
AND FOCUS ON WHAT I CAN."
ROBERT M. HENSEL—FAMOUS INSPIRATIONAL QUOTES

# NOTE TO SELF
## DISCOVERING YOUR PURPOSE AS YOU
## NAVIGATE THE UNKNOWN

_____

_____

_____

_____

_____

_____

_____

_____

_____

_____

_____

_____

_____

_____

_____

_____

_____

_____

_____

_____

"YOU PUT YOUR INTENTION AND YOUR ATTENTION ON
WHAT IT IS THAT YOU WANT TO SHIFT AND CHANGE."
WAYNE DYER—FAMOUS INSPIRATIONAL QUOTES

# CHAPTER 16

# PRAISE FOR DELIVERANCE

"I WILL PRAISE YOU, O LORD MY GOD, WITH ALL MY
HEART; I WILL GLORIFY YOUR NAME FOREVER. FOR GREAT
IS YOUR LOVE TOWARD ME; YOU HAVE DELIVERED ME
FROM THE DEPTS, FROM THE REALM OF THE DEAD."
PSALM 86:12-13 (NIV)

Now that you have navigated the unknown and you can say for
sure that God is your "refuge and strength, a very present help in
trouble". You can give Him praise. Your All-Sufficient One, your
Rock took care of you. He gave you sight when you were blind and
delivered you from the depths of darkness into the light. Through
His awesome power, He navigated you to a safe place. On your own
you could do nothing. You would have stayed in the same place, gone
round and round trying to move from here to there with no luck. It
was when you turn your situation over to God that you could see
progress in your life. It is because God loves you so much. He filled
you up with His overflowing love and gave you His strength and His
compassion.

He melded your spirit and your will with His and they became
one. His love and faithfulness are tremendous. So now praise Him

with your lips, your voice, and your mouth. Praise Him with your whole heart. Let Him know that you want to become less, so that He can become more in your life. Ask Him to lead you to the front of eternal blessings and give Him thanks for saving your soul and for using you for His purpose.

"Let God change your life. First of all, let Him give you a new mind. Then you will know what God wants you to do. And the things you do will be good pleasing and perfect.

# Notes To Self
## Praise for Deliverance

_____

_____

_____

_____

_____

_____

_____

_____

_____

_____

_____

_____

_____

_____

_____

_____

_____

_____

_____

_____

_____

_____

_____

_____

NOTES TO SELF
PRAISE FOR DELIVERANCE

## CHAPTER 17

# DO YOU HAVE A RELATIONSHIP WITH JESUS?

"I AM THE VINE; YOU ARE THE BRANCHES. IF A MAN
REMAINS IN ME AND I IN HIM, HE WILL BEAR MUCH
FRUIT; APART FROM ME YOU CAN DO NOTHING."
JOHN 15:5 (NIV)

God loves you! He created you to be a special, unique, one-of-a-kind individual, and He has a specific purpose and plan for your life. And through a personal relationship with your Creator, God, you can discover a way of life that will truly bless your soul. It does not matter who you are, where you have been, or what you have done, or even where you are in your life right now, God's love and grace are greater than any sin you may have committed. Jesus gave His life so you can receive forgiveness from God and have a new life. He is waiting for you to invite Him into your life to be your Lord and Savior. If you have committed your life to Him and are following Him, all you need to do is ask Him for forgiveness of your sins, and to give you the kind of life you are seeking and pray this prayer.

Lord Jesus, thank you for giving your life for me and forgiving me of my sins, so that I can have a personal relationship with you.

I am sorry for the mistakes I have made in my life, and I know I need you to live a better life. You said in Romans 10:9 that, "If thou confess with thy mouth the Lord Jesus Christ, and shalt believe in thine heart that God hath raised him from the dead, thou shalt be saved." I believe that you are the Son of God and I confess that you are my Lord and Savior. Thank you for giving me a fresh start, and a new life. Amen.

It is good to know that God loves us so much! He wants to have a deep, intimate relationship with you that grows every day as you spend time with Him in Bible Study and in prayer. "Make a decision right now to believe God more than you believe how you feel, what you want, or what you think." I want to encourage and congratulate you as you go forth in your new life in Christ.

However, during your Christian walk with God, one of the most important words that you will need to embrace is the word faith. You see, to build a solid relationship with God, all believers must believe in God, and that He can do whatever He says He will do. Because the faith you have in God must be unshakable or the constant trials and tribulations from the enemy will turn you away from God.

The Bible says in Ephesians 2:8-9, "For by grace are ye saved through faith; and that not of yourselves: it is the gift of God: Not of works, lest any man should boast." This scripture can be interpreted as saying that the grace that comes from loving God has been given to mankind as a free gift or unmerited favor.

In your Christian walk, your faith will constantly be challenged to act or display behavior that is not in the norm. But Christians sometimes make mistakes; just ask God for His forgiveness and keep moving. 1 Peter 2:9 tells us that, "But ye are a chosen generation, a royal priesthood, an holy nation, a peculiar people; that ye should shew forth the praises of Him who hath called you out of darkness into His marvelous light." Also, prayer is a very effective part of your relationship with God, but God will not be mocked. You cannot go out and live any way you please and expect to have a Holy God respond to your prayers.

Melvin Douglas Wilson, writer of "*The Good Book*" states, "The process of sanctification is the season of life when you must embrace and celebrate the ideas of total change from the old person that took on the ways of this world to a new person who is now ready to live the good life for God and be free from bondage of sin." Therefore, please keep your eyes on the prize. Do not take your eyes off your relationship with Jesus Christ because you do not want to lose what you have gained in your relationship with Him.

2 Corinthians 7:1 says, "Having therefore these promises, dearly beloved, let us cleanse ourselves from all filthiness of the flesh and spirit, perfecting holiness in the fear of God."

# NOTE TO SELF
## DO YOU HAVE A RELATIONSHIP WITH JESUS?

# NOTE TO SELF
## DO YOU HAVE A RELATIONSHIP WITH JESUS?

# CHAPTER 18

# CHRISTIAN RESPONSIBILITIES

"LET US HEAR THE CONCLUSION OF THE WHOLE
MATTER: FEAR GOD AND KEEP HIS COMMANDMENTS:
FOR THIS IS THE WHOLE DUTY OF MAN."
(ECCLESIASTES 12:13 KJV)

First, we have a Christian duty to serve and help others. The Bible says, "Each one should use whatever gift he has received to serve others, faithfully administering God's grace in various form." Actually, 1 Peter 4:10NIV tells us, "God has given each of you a gift from His great variety of spiritual gifts. Use them well to serve one another." We must fully understand that until the Lord returns there are souls to reach and ministries of every sort to be performed."

When you live by the Spirit's power, you will want to be of spiritual help to others. You will not be harshly critical when you see other believers caught in wrongdoing but will feel the sorrow of others as if it were your own. You will remember how easily someone can be overcome by temptation. It is said that people are foolish when they compare themselves with others in order to feel satisfied about their own spirituality. Each person is answerable to God for his or her own behavior, regardless of what other people may have done to them. We are responsible for our money, time and energy, talents, bodies, minds, spirits, and we should invest in nothing that does not in some way contribute to the work of the Lord.

Also, Christians should help financially support their church or their ministry. Christians, like a farmer, reap what they sow. On the other hand, if they put God's affairs before their own, their lives will produce qualities of eternal value. This is the season for sowing, not reaping. By helping others, whether financially or otherwise, believers guarantee for themselves future reward of lasting worth.

Simply put, our responsibility as believers lies in working for the Lord, whether it is in caring for orphans and widows, giving to the hungry or the naked, visiting the sick and those in prison. We as believers have God's own promises that our work will not be in vain. Because it is the Lord Jesus Christ you are serving.

Obligations Christian have:

- Obey the scriptures (John 14:15, 21, 23).
- Embrace the Word of God.
- Walk in the same manner as Christ walked (1 John 2:6).
- Love one another (2 John 6).
- Walk in the truth (3 John 4).
- Pray without ceasing for instruction and guidance (1 Thessalonians 5: 17-18)
- Honor God and His word (Neh. 8:5-6).
- Study (2 Timothy 2:15).

When we believe Jesus and accept His death and resurrection, we will begin to allow God to instill in us a desire to obey Him. Our motivation and our responsibilities begin to look like walking with Jesus.

1 John 5:1-3 also tells us, "Everyone who believes that Jesus is the Christ is born of God, and everyone who loves the father loves His child as well. This is how we know that we love the children of God: by loving God and carrying out His command. This is love for God: to obey His command. And His commands are not burdensome, for everyone born of God overcomes the world."

Finally, as believers, 1 Corinthians 15:58 says "Therefore, my beloved brethren, be ye steadfast, unmovable, always abounding in the work of the Lord, forasmuch as ye know that your labour is not in vain in the Lord."

# NOTE TO SELF
## CHRISTIAN RESPONSIBILITIES

# Note to Self
## Christian Responsibilities

# CHAPTER 19

# WHAT I KNOW FOR SURE

"FOR GOD SO LOVED THE WORLD THAT HE GAVE HIS
ONE AND ONLY SON, THAT WHOEVER BELIEVES IN
HIM SHALL NOT PERISH BUT HAVE ETERNAL LIFE."
JOHN 3:16 (NIV)

I know for sure that God's word is true. He will never leave us nor forsake us. When we allow Him to take control of our lives, He will navigate us to those plans and promises that He said He has for us. He says in Jeremiah 29:11, "For I know the plans I have for you, "declares the Lord, "plans to prosper you and not to harm you, plans to give you hope and a future."

As Shepherd and Lord over our lives, He will take us through the green pastures, He will lead us beside the still waters, He will be with us even in death—death of a loved one, friend, or acquaintance. His goodness and mercy will follow us all the days of our lives. Those plans and promises to us He will safely keep until He arrives ready to bring us home with Him.

Throughout scriptures, God is referred to as the Good Shepherd, the Great Shepherd, the Chief Shepherd, and even "The Gate." We, His sheep, referred to as dependent on the shepherd for our provision, guidance, and protection because the Good Shepherd, the Great Shepherd, the Chief Shepherd lays down His life for His sheep. Once you commit your life to the Good Shepherd and become one with Him, He knows your name. He says in in John 10:14, that "I know my sheep, and my sheep know me."

When you recognize the Good Shepherd, and commit your life, follow Him! Because our going in and out, living life day by day is in His hands. When you allow God our Shepherd, to guide you, you will have peace and contentment. As the Lord is the Good Shepherd, so we are His sheep, not dumb, frightened, timid, passive, wayward animals, but obedient, loving followers. Our shepherd knows the "green pastures" and "still waters" that restore us, and we will reach these places only by following Him obediently.

# NOTE TO SELF
## WHAT I KNOW FOR SURE

_____

_____

_____

_____

_____

_____

_____

_____

_____

_____

_____

_____

_____

_____

_____

_____

_____

_____

_____

_____

# NOTE TO SELF
## WHAT I KNOW FOR SURE

_____
_____
_____
_____
_____
_____
_____
_____
_____
_____
_____
_____
_____
_____
_____
_____
_____
_____
_____
_____
_____
_____
_____
_____
_____
_____
_____
_____

# SCRIPTURES

### Psalm 23 (KJV)

"The LORD is my shepherd; I shall not want. He maketh me to lie down in green pastures: He he leadeth me beside the still waters. He restoreth my soul: He he leadeth me in the paths of righteousness for his His name's sake. Yea, though I walk through the valley of the shadow of death, I will fear no evil: for thou art with me; thy rod and thy staff they comfort me. Thou preparest a table before me in the presence of mine enemies: thou anointers my head with oil; my cup runneth over. Surely goodness and mercy shall follow me all the days of my life: and I will dwell in the house of the LORD forever."

### Psalm 24:1-10 (KJV)

"The earth is the Lord's, and the fulness thereof; the world, and they that dwell therein. For He hath founded it upon the seas and established it upon the floods. Who shall ascend into the hill of the Lord? Or who shall stand in His holy place? He that hath clean hands, and a pure heart; who hath not lift up His soul unto vanity; nor sworn deceitfully. He shall receive the blessing from the Lord, and righteousness from the God of His salvation. This is the generation of them that seek Him, that seek thy face, O Jacob, Selah. Lift up your heads, O ye gates; and be ye lift up; ye everlasting doors, and the King of glory shall come in. Who is this King of glory? The Lord strong and mighty, the Lord mighty in battle. Lift up your heads, O ye gates; even lift them up, ye everlasting doors, and the king of glory shall come in. Who is this King of glory? The Lord of hosts, He is the king of glory. Selah".

## Psalm 63 (HCSB)

"God, You are my God; I Eagerly seek You. I thirst for You; my body faints for You in a land that is dry, desolate, and without water. So, I gaze on You in the sanctuary to see Your Strength and Your glory. My lips will glorify You because Your faithful love is better than life. So I will praise You as long as I live; at Your name, I will lift up my hands. You satisfy me as with rich food; my mouth will praise You with joyful lips. When I think of You as I on my bed, I meditate on You during the night watches because You are my helper, I will rejoice in the shadow of Your wings. I follow close to You; Your right hand holds on to me. But those who seek to destroy my life, will go into the depts of the earth. They will be given over to the power of the sword; they will become the jackal's prey. But the king will rejoice in God; all who swears by Him will boast, for the mouth of liars will be shut."

## Psalm 121 (KJV)

"I lift up mine eyes unto the hills, from whence cometh my help. My help cometh from the LORD, which made heaven and earth. He will not suffer my foot to be moved: He that keepeth thee will not slumber. Behold, He that keepeth Israel shall neither slumber nor sleep. The LORD is thy keeper: the Lord is thy shade upon thy right hand. The sun shall not smite thee by day, nor the moon by night. The Lord shall preserve thee from evil: He shall preserve thy soul.

The Lord shall preserve thy going out and thy coming in from this time forth, and even for evermore."

## Isaiah 43: 1-4 (KJV)

"But now thus saith the LORD that created thee, O Jacob, and He that formed thee, O Israel, Fear not: for I have redeemed thee, I have called thee by thy name; thou art mine. When thou passest through the waters, I will be with thee; and through the rivers, they shall not overflow thee: when thou walkest through the fire, thou shall not be burned; neither shall the flame kindle upon thee. For I am the LORD thy God, the Holy One of Israel, thy Savior: I gave Egypt for thy ransom, Ethiopia and Seba for thee. Since thou wast precious in my sight, thou hast been honorable, and I have loved thee: therefore will I give men for thee, and people for thy life."

## Galatians 6:9 (KJV)

"And let us not be weary in well doing for in due season we shall reap if we faint not."

# JOURNALING

Journaling is a profound tool for enhancing your spiritual journey, and it can allow you to get to the heart of what you see inside of yourself. There is no right or wrong answers. As you journal, just be honest with yourself and with God, and you will be sure to find what you are looking for. After reading *Navigating the Unknown: Trusting God with the Results*, hopefully you will understand yourself better.

_____

_____

_____

_____

_____

_____

_____

_____

_____

_____

_____

_____

_____

"AND MY GOD WILL SUPPLY ALL YOUR NEEDS ACCORDING
TO HIS RICHES IN GLORY IN CHRIST JESUS,", WHAT
HE HAS IN MIND FOR YOU IS IMMEASURABLY BETTER
THAN WHAT YOU HAVE LOST OR GIVEN UP.
PHILIPPIANS 4:19

_____
_____
_____
_____
_____
_____
_____
_____
_____
_____
_____
_____
_____
_____
_____
_____
_____
_____
_____

"BUT YOU ARE A CHOSEN GENERATION, A ROYAL
PRIESTHOOD, A HOLY NATION, HIS OWN SPECIAL
PEOPLE, THAT YOU MAY PROCLAIM THE PRAISES OF
HIM, WHO CALLED YOU OUT OF DARKNESS INTO HIS
MARVELOUS LIGHT". WRITE DOWN THE STRUGGLES
GOD HAS HELPED YOU THROUGH, AND HOW YOU
HAVE BEEN MADE A NEW CREATURE IN CHRIST."
1 PETER 2:9 (ESV)

THROUGHOUT THE BIBLE, GOD SAYS YOU ARE
LOVED. JOURNAL FOUR DECLARATIONS THAT WILL
REMIND YOU THAT YOU ARE HIS BELOVED. AFFIRM
YOURSELF DAILY AND PRAY EVERY MORNING
THAT HIS TRUTH WILL BE SHOWN TO YOU.

"ABOVE ALL, TAKING THE SHIELD OF FAITH, WHEREWITH YE SHALL BE ABLE TO QUENCH ALL THE FIERY DARTS OF THE WICKED ONE." FAITH GUIDES YOU IN YOUR DAILY WALK. WHEN YOU HONESTLY BELIEVE THAT YOU HAVE BEEN MADE RIGHT WITH GOD THROUGH FAITH IN CHRIST, YOU CAN OVERCOME FEELINGS OF GUILT AND SHAME. (EPHESIAN 6:16 KJV)

"BUT BE DOERS OF THE WORD, AND NOT HEARERS ONLY,
DECEIVING YOURSELVES. FOR IF ANYONE IS A HEARER
OF THE WORD AND NOT A DOER, HE IS LIKE A MAN WHO
LOOKS INTENTLY AT HIS NATURAL FACE IN A MIRROR.
FOR HE LOOKS AT HIMSELF AND GOES AWAY AND AT
ONCE FORGETS WHAT HE WAS LIKE. BUT THE ONE WHO
LOOKS INTO THE PERFECT LAW, THE LAW OF LIBERTY,
AND PRESERVES, BEING NO HEARER WHO FORGETS BUT A
DOER WHO ACTS, HE WILL BE BLESSED IN HIS DOING."
JAMES 1:22-25 (ESV)

"NOW IF WE ARE CHILDREN, THEN WE ARE HEIRS OF GOD AND CO-HEIRS WITH CHRIST, IF INDEED WE SHARE IN HIS SUFFERINGS IN ORDER THAT WE MAY ALSO SHARE IN HIS GLORY." WRITE THIS VERSE IN YOUR OWN WORDS AND MEDITATE DAILY ON THE FACT THAT YOUR INHERITANCE IN GOD IS GREATER THAN ANY TROUBLE YOU MAY ENDURE. ROMANS 8:17 (NIV)

_____

_____

_____

_____

_____

_____

_____

_____

_____

_____

_____

_____

_____

_____

_____

_____

_____

_____

_____

_____

_____

"NO, IN ALL THESE THINGS WE ARE MORE THAN CONQUERORS THROUGH HIM WHO LOVES US." WHAT DO YOU THINK IT MEANS TO BE MORE THAN A CONQUEROR IN CHRIST? DO YOU BELIEVE THIS ABOUT YOURSELF? JOURNAL ABOUT WHY OR WHY NOT AND WRITE A PRAYER ASKING GOD TO INCREASE YOUR FAITH SO YOU CAN SEE YOURSELF AS A CONQUEROR. ROMANS 8:37 (NIV)

_____

_____

_____

_____

_____

_____

_____

_____

_____

_____

_____

_____

_____

_____

_____

_____

_____

_____

_____

According to the scriptures, we are to be, "Rooted and built up in Him, strengthen in the faith as you were taught, and overflowing with thankfulness." Write down the scriptures that roots you, and journal about at least three things for which you are grateful for.
Colossians 2:7 (NIV)

_____
_____
_____
_____
_____
_____
_____
_____
_____
_____
_____
_____
_____
_____
_____
_____
_____
_____
_____
_____
_____

"AND THEY OVERCAME HIM BY THE BLOOD OF THE LAMB, AND BY THE WORD OF THEIR TESTIMONY" HAVE YOU SHARED YOUR TESTIMONY WITH ANYONE SINCE READING *NAVIGATING THE UNKNOWN: TRUSTING GOD WITH THE RESULTS*? HAS IT CHANGED AT ALL? WRITE ABOUT IT HERE AND FOCUS ON YOUR PROGRESS, INSTEAD OF HOW FAR YOU NEED TO GO. REVELATION 12:11A (KJV)

"AND THE LORD SHALL MAKE THEE THE HEAD, AND
NOT THE TAIL;  AND THOU SHALT BE ABOVE ONLY, AND
THOU SHALT NOT BENEATH." WRITE ABOUT FIVE THINGS
YOU ARE NOT. LOOK AT THE FIVE THINGS. WHAT DO
THESE THINGS SAY ABOUT YOU AND YOUR JOURNEY?
DEUTERONOMY 28:13A (KJV)

WHAT ARE YOUR HOPES AND DESIRES FOR THE FUTURE,
AS JESUS MENDS YOUR PAIN AND SUFFERING? FOR
WHAT DO YOU LONG? ASK GOD TO GUIDE YOU AND
GIVE HIM THE GLORY FOR FUTURE BLESSINGS.

_____
_____
_____
_____
_____
_____
_____
_____
_____
_____
_____
_____
_____
_____
_____
_____
_____
_____
_____
_____
_____
_____

When we give our lives to the Lord, we will still have trials and tribulations. James 1:2-4 tell us to, "Consider it pure joy, my brothers, whenever you face trials of many kinds, because you know that the testing of your faith develops perseverance. Perseverance must finish its works so that you may be mature and complete, lacking anything." I encourage you to search the scriptures so that you will be prepared to defeat the enemy when he comes against you.
James 1: 2-4 (NIV)

_____

_____

_____

_____

_____

_____

_____

_____

_____

_____

_____

_____

_____

_____

_____

_____

"ASK AND IT SHALL BE GIVEN TO YOU;  SEEK AND YOU WILL
FIND;  KNOCK AND IT WILL BE OPENED TO YOU." "ALWAYS
PRAY TO GOD ABOUT WHAT IS GOING ON IN YOUR LIFE."
MATTHEW 7:7 (ESV)

_____
_____
_____
_____
_____
_____
_____
_____
_____
_____
_____
_____
_____
_____
_____
_____
_____
_____
_____
_____
_____
_____
_____

# YOUR JOURNEY

My prayer for you is that after reading this book you will find your feet planted just a little more firmly on the ground. That even though the unknown can be scary, when you put your trust in God, you can find joy and peace. Also, I pray that God's promises of protection give you something else to stand on when fearful and anxious thoughts come to you. I encourage you to fight to keep God's word in the forefront of your mind.

As you journey, may God's word come alive for you in all you do. Ask Him to show off! Let Him know that you need His promises of protection to help you survive. I know without a doubt that He will show up. As you move away from fear and guilt into God's peace, may your story of redemption take you headfirst into the loving, powerful, and trustworthy truth of God's word. Go forth, Navigate the Unknown, and trust God With the Results.

# PRAYER

Father God, I thank you that you do not leave us in this life to journey alone. I thank you that you give us promises that are trustworthy and true, I pray for the courage to believe in your word more than anything else. I pray that you continue to bring discipline to our minds so that when fear and turmoil come to us, we have your word to stand on. Help us find a way to remember what you have said to us.

May you perform miracles in our minds and in our hearts as you bring the right Bible scriptures to us exactly when we need them the most. I pray that as people come to you for help you will do for them that you have done for me. Help them see more clearly than they ever have seen before, and may they be open to your promises in a whole new and life-giving way. Thank you for your power, you might, your love, and your generosity in all things. Amen.

# ABOUT THE AUTHOR

Born and raised in a small town in Alabama, Annie relocated to Middletown, Connecticut, in 1968 and then to Hartford, Connecticut, in 1970. She currently serves as an Associate Minister at Agape Fellowship Ministries and Outreach. She serves as Director of Christian Education, and she teaches new member's Class and adult Sunday School. Annie serves on the greeters and health committee, and she is the Chairperson of the Agape Fellowship Ministries Scholarship Program. Annie is the Secretary for New Life 4 US Outreach Ministries. This ministry is responsible for mentoring students between ages 8 and 15 years. Annie serves as Liaison between Agape Fellowship Ministries and (EHIM) East Hartford Interfaith Ministries, helping define the needs within the church and the community. She participates in the Building Bountiful Friendship ministry and has been the Secretary for the group for the past five years. Annie is part of Women for Christ Outreach Ministries helping to implement training and fundraising efforts to provide funding for youth conferences and other activities. She plans and help organize Clergy and Leadership Conferences for the ministry as well.

In 2015 Annie retired after more than thirty years of service from the State of Connecticut as an Office Supervisor. In 2019, she received her Doctor of Divinity Degree from Heart Bible Institute University. Annie is blessed with two beautiful and amazing children. Shawn and Kristin... Annie has two stepchildren Karl and Tangie. She has five grandkids, three great-grandkids, and six step grandchildren. She is married to Curtis a man after God's own heart. Annie's passion to help others led her to author this book.